Windows® Internet Explorer® 8

ILLUSTRATED

ESSENTIALS

Katherine T. Pinard

COURSE TECHNOLOGY
CENGAGE Learning

Australia • Canada • Mexico • Singapore • Spain • United Kingdom • United States

COURSE TECHNOLOGY
CENGAGE Learning™

Windows Internet Explorer 8—Illustrated Essentials
Katherine T. Pinard

Executive Editor: Marjorie Hunt

Senior Product Manager: Christina Kling Garrett

Associate Acquisitions Editor: Brandi Shailer

Associate Product Manager: Michelle Camisa

Editorial Assistant: Kim Klasner

Director of Marketing: Cheryl Costantini

Marketing Manager: Ryan DeGrote

Marketing Coordinator: Kristen Panciocco

Developmental Editor: Kim T. M. Crowley

Content Project Manager: Matthew Hutchinson

Art Director: Jill Ort

Proofreader: Harry Johnson

Indexer: Liz Cunningham

QA Manuscript Reviewer: John Frietas

Print Buyer: Fola Orekoya

Cover Designers: Elizabeth Paquin, Kathleen Fivel, Marissa Falco

Cover Artist: Mark Hunt

Composition: GEX Publishing Services

For product information and technology assistance, contact us at
Cengage Learning Customer & Sales Support, 1-800-354-9706

For permission to use material from this text or product, submit all requests online at **cengage.com/permissions**

Further permissions questions can be emailed to
permissionrequest@cengage.com

Microsoft and the Office logo are either registered trademarks or trademarks of Microsoft Corporation in the United States and/or other countries. Thomson Course Technology is an independent entity from Microsoft Corporation, and not affiliated with Microsoft in any manner. Microsoft product screen shots reprinted with permission from Microsoft Corporation.

ISBN-13: 978-0-538-74485-0

ISBN-10: 0-538-74485-5

Course Technology
20 Channel Center Street
Boston, MA 02210
USA

Cengage Learning is a leading provider of customized learning solutions with office locations around the globe, including Singapore, the United Kingdom, Australia, Mexico, Brazil, and Japan. Locate your local office at:
international.cengage.com/region

Cengage Learning produ cts are represented in Canada by Nelson Education, Ltd.

To learn more about Course Technology, visit **www.cengage.com/coursetechnology**

To learn more about Cengage Learning, visit **www.cengage.com**

Purchase any of our products at your local college store or at our preferred online store **www.ichapters.com**

Printed in the United States of America
1 2 3 4 5 6 15 14 13 12 11 10

About This Book

Welcome to *Windows Internet Explorer 8 — Illustrated Essentials*! Since 1994, millions of students have used various Illustrated Series texts to master software skills and learn computer concepts. We are proud to bring you this textbook on Internet Explorer 8, Microsoft's market leading Internet browser that offers new security features designed to keep you, your personal information, and your computer safe while surfing the Web.

In addition to covering basic browsing and searching skills, this book also covers the newest features of Windows Internet Explorer 8 including the following:

- **Accelerators:** The new Accelerators feature lets you look up contextual information about a particular item on a page. Accelerators make searching for information easier, because you have immediate access to related information without having to link to another page. For example, if you select the name of a restaurant on a Web page, the Live Search Map Accelerator opens a Windows Live Search map so you can immediately see the location of the restaurant.

- **Web Slices:** Web Slices allow you to subscribe to specific content on a Web page, making it possible to stay up to date with this content, such as headlines or weather in a particular city.

- **Search box:** The improved Search box now provides suggested results and suggested search expressions based on text you enter in it.

We are confident that this books and all its available resources will help your students master the basics of using Internet Explorer 8, and will give them a solid foundation for all of their Web browsing.

Author Acknowledgments

Thank you very much to Marjorie Hunt who gave me the opportunity to write this book, to Michelle Camisa, who did a fantastic job keeping this, her first project, flowing smoothly even when the author let things fall through the cracks. Thank you also to John Freitas with his keen eye for catching errors and diplomatic phrasing for pointing them out. Special thanks to Kim Crowley, who, as always, gave sage advice in all areas and polished my writing. Finally, thank you to Angela Binda, who supported me and led me in Assertiveness Training 101 over the years when I needed it.

—**Katherine T. Pinard**

This edition is dedicated to the memory of Joseph B. Dougherty, the first Publisher of Course Technology.

Preface

Welcome to *Windows Internet Explorer 8—Illustrated Essentials*. If this is your first experience with the Illustrated series, you'll see that this book has a unique design: each skill is presented on two facing pages, with steps on the left and screens on the right. The layout makes it easy to digest a skill without having to read a lot of text and flip pages to see an illustration.

This book is an ideal learning tool for a wide range of learners—the "rookies" will find the clean design easy to follow and focused with only essential information presented, and the "hot-shots" will appreciate being able to move quickly through the lessons to find the information they need without reading a lot of text. The design also makes this a great reference after the course is over! See the illustration on the right to learn more about the pedagogical and design elements of a typical lesson.

What's New in This Edition

We've made many changes and enhancements to this edition to make it the best ever. Here are some highlights of what's new:

- **New Content** — Completely updated to cover the new elements of Internet Explorer 8, including the new search and private browsing features.
- **Hot Topics** — With lessons on both Accelerators and Web Slices, this edition covers all the hot new features your students will need to know about.
- **Case Study** — Quest Specialty Travel, an adventure, culture, and educational travel company provides a practical scenario for students as they learn skills.

Each two-page spread focuses on a single skill.

Concise text introduces the basic principles in the lesson and integrates a real-world case study.

UNIT
A
Internet Explorer

Using Tabbed Browsing

Tabbed browsing allows you to open multiple Web pages in the browser window. The title of the Web page appears on the tab itself, and the Web page appears in the window below the tab. To open a new Web page without closing the current page, you open a new tab and load the new Web page in that tab. The tab that is on top is called the **active tab**. When you open multiple tabs, they are automatically sorted into **tab groups**, collections of related tabs. The tabs in a tab group all appear in the same color so that you can easily see which tabs are related to each other. You decide to explain tabbed browsing next so that the employees can jump quickly from one Web page to another.

STEPS

1. **Point to the** New Tab button **to the right of the Quest Specialty Travel :: Destinations tab so that the New Tab icon appears on it, then click**
   A new tab opens on top of the Destinations page and the New Tab button shifts to the right. The new tab contains links for reopening closed tabs and the previous browsing session, and for accessing new features in Internet Explorer 8. The Quick Tabs button and the Tab List arrow appear to the left of the first tab. See Figure A-11. Notice the text in the Address bar is selected.

   TROUBLE
   If a dialog box opens asking if you want to install Microsoft Silverlight, click No thanks.

2. **Type** microsoft.com, **then click the** Go button
   The text you typed replaces the selected text in the Address bar, and the home page on the Microsoft Web site opens in the new tab.

3. **Click the** Quest Specialty Travel :: Destinations tab
   The Destinations page on the Quest Web site becomes the active tab.

4. **Right-click the** Quest logo **in the upper left of the Web page, then click** Open Link in New Tab **on the shortcut menu**
   The Quest logo is a link to the Quest Specialty Travel home page. A new tab opens behind the current tab—that is, between the Destinations and the Microsoft page—and the Quest home page loads in that tab. Because you opened the new tab by right-clicking a link, the tabs for the two Quest pages are colored green to indicate that they belong to the same tab group.

5. **Right-click the** About Us link, **and then click** Open Link in New Tab
   A third Quest Specialty Travel tab opens. As you add tabs, the tabs shrink and you can't see the complete page name on each tab.

   QUICK TIP
   You can change the tab order by dragging a tab left or right to a new position on the Tab row.

6. **Point to the** leftmost Quest tab **to see a ScreenTip that identifies it as the Destinations page, then click the** middle Quest tab
   The tab displaying the home page for the Quest Specialty Travel Web site appears in the browser window. The other Quest Specialty Travel pages and the Microsoft page are hidden behind the current Web page.

7. **Click the** Tab List arrow **immediately to the left of the first tab on the Tab row**
   A list of currently open tabs appears. A check mark appears next to Quest Specialty Travel, which indicates that this is the page displayed on the active tab. The faint horizontal line above Microsoft Corporation separates the two tab groups.

   QUICK TIP
   Click the Quick Tabs button to the left of the first tab to display thumbnail images depicting each of the open tab in the window.

8. **Click** Microsoft Corporation **in the list**
   The third tab becomes the active tab.

9. **Click the** Quest Specialty Travel tab (the middle one), **then right-click that tab**
   A shortcut menu opens containing commands for working with tabs. See Table A-3 for a description of these commands.

10. **Click** Ungroup This Tab **on the shortcut menu**
    The tab is recolored white to indicate that it is no longer part of the tab group whose tabs are colored green, and it is shifted to the right so it is no longer located in the middle of the tab group. See Figure A-12.

Internet 12   Getting Started with Internet Explorer 8

Hints as well as troubleshooting tips appear, right where you need them—next to the step itself.

Every lesson features large, full-color representations of what the screen should look like as students complete the numbered steps.

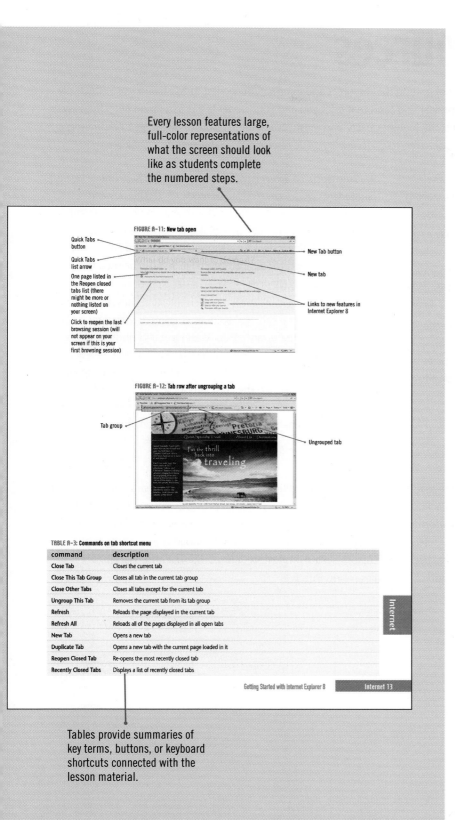

FIGURE A-11: New tab open

Quick Tabs button
Quick Tabs list arrow
One page listed in the Reopen closed tabs list (there might be more or nothing listed on your screen)
Click to reopen the last browsing session (will not appear on your screen if this is your first browsing session)

New Tab button
New tab
Links to new features in Internet Explorer 8

FIGURE A-12: Tab row after ungrouping a tab

Tab group
Ungrouped tab

TABLE A-3: Commands on tab shortcut menu

command	description
Close Tab	Closes the current tab
Close This Tab Group	Closes all tab in the current tab group
Close Other Tabs	Closes all tabs except for the current tab
Ungroup This Tab	Removes the current tab from its tab group
Refresh	Reloads the page displayed in the current tab
Refresh All	Reloads all of the pages displayed in all open tabs
New Tab	Opens a new tab
Duplicate Tab	Opens a new tab with the current page loaded in it
Reopen Closed Tab	Re-opens the most recently closed tab
Recently Closed Tabs	Displays a list of recently closed tabs

Getting Started with Internet Explorer 8   Internet 13

Tables provide summaries of key terms, buttons, or keyboard shortcuts connected with the lesson material.

Assignments

The lessons use Quest Specialty Travel, a fictional adventure travel company, as the case study. The assignments on the light purple pages at the end of each unit increase in difficulty. Assignments include:

- **Concepts Reviews** include multiple choice, matching, and screen identification questions.

- **Skills Reviews** provide additional hands-on, step-by-step reinforcement.

- **Independent Challenges** are case projects requiring critical thinking and application of the unit skills. The Independent Challenges increase in difficulty, with the first one in each unit being the easiest. Independent Challenges 2 and 3 become increasingly open-ended, requiring more independent problem solving.

- **Real Life Independent Challenges** are practical exercises in which students work in a way that will help them with their every day lives.

- **Advanced Challenge Exercises** set within the Independent Challenges provide optional steps for more advanced students.

- **Visual Workshops** are practical, self-graded capstone projects that require independent problem solving.

Instructor Resources

The Instructor Resources CD is Course Technology's way of putting the resources and information needed to teach and learn effectively into your hands. With an integrated array of teaching and learning tools that offer you and your students a broad range of technology-based instructional options, we believe this CD represents the highest quality and most cutting edge resources available to instructors today. Many of these resources are available at *www.cengage.com/coursetechnology*. The resources available with this book are:

- **Instructor's Manual**—Available as an electronic file, the Instructor's Manual includes detailed lecture topics with teaching tips for each unit.
- **Sample Syllabus**—Prepare and customize your course easily using this sample course outline.
- **PowerPoint Presentations**—Each unit has a corresponding PowerPoint presentation that you can use in lecture, distribute to your students, or customize to suit your course.
- **Figure Files**—The figures in the text are provided on the Instructor Resources CD to help you illustrate key topics or concepts. You can create traditional overhead transparencies by printing the figure files. Or you can create electronic slide shows by using the figures in a presentation program such as PowerPoint.

- **Solutions to Exercises**—Solutions to Exercises contains every file students are asked to create or modify in the lessons and end-of-unit material. Also provided in this section is a document outlining the solutions for the end-of-unit Concepts Review, Skills Review, and Independent Challenges. An Annotated Solution File and Grading Rubric accompany each file and can be used together for quick and easy grading.
- **ExamView**—ExamView is a powerful testing software package that allows you to create and administer printed, computer (LAN-based), and Internet exams. ExamView includes hundreds of questions that correspond to the topics covered in this text, enabling students to generate detailed study guides that include page references for further review. The computer-based and Internet testing components allow students to take exams at their computers, and also saves you time by grading each exam automatically.

Content for Online Learning

Course Technology has partnered with Blackboard, the leading distance learning solution provider and class-management platform today. In addition to providing content for Blackboard and WebCT, Course Technology provides premium online content for multiple learning management system platforms. To access this material, simply visit our password-protected instructor resources available at *www.cengage.com/coursetechnology*. The resources available for download may include topic reviews, case projects, review questions, test banks, practice tests, custom syllabi, and more. For additional information or for an instructor username and password, please contact your sales representative.

Contents

Getting Started with Internet Explorer 8

Windows Internet Explorer is a program you use to examine and interact with files on the World Wide Web. This unit introduces you to the Internet and the World Wide Web and teaches you how to use Internet Explorer to navigate the Web. You will also learn how to return to pages you have already viewed, how to view more than one place on the Web at a time, how to print a page from the Web, how to get help, and how to exit Internet Explorer. 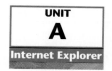 Quest Specialty Travel is expanding and has just purchased Sheehan Tours, an established travel agency in Boston, Massachusetts. Although each member of the Sheehan Tours staff has a computer on his or her desk, the staff shares a centrally located computer in the office to connect to the Internet. To promote efficiency, you install new computer equipment and connect all of the computers to the Internet. You soon discover that many of the employees never learned how to browse the Internet comfortably. Your task is to teach the staff how to use Internet Explorer.

OBJECTIVES

Understand Web browsing

Start Windows Internet Explorer 8

Explore the program window

Find and navigate a Web site

Navigate to previously visited
   Web pages

Use tabbed browsing

Save a Web page

Print a Web page

Get Help

Close tabs and exit Internet Explorer

Understanding Web Browsing

The **Internet** connects computers all over the world using telephone lines, fiber-optic cables, satellites, and other telecommunications media. The **World Wide Web** (**WWW** or **Web**) is a subset of the Internet composed of files in a special format that allows them to be connected to each other. ▰▰▰▰ Before you can teach the staff how to explore the Internet, they need to understand some basic terminology associated with the Internet and the Web.

DETAILS

Before you start exploring the Internet, you should understand the following terms:

- Web page

  A **Web page** is a specially formatted file designed for use on the Web. A Web page typically includes text and graphics as well as ways to connect to other Web pages. It might also include audio and video clips. An example of a Web page is shown in Figure A-1.

- Web site

  A **Web site** is a collection of related Web pages stored on a Web server. A **Web server** is a computer or a network of computers that stores Web pages and makes them available on the Web. The Web page shown in Figure A-1 is one page on the Web site of the U.S. Library of Congress. The main page around which a Web site is built is called the **home page**.

- Web browser

  A **Web browser** (**browser**) is software that allows you to navigate to, open, view, and interact with files on the Web. Internet Explorer is a popular Web browser that comes installed with Windows. Using a browser to look for and view Web pages is called **browsing** or, more popularly, **surfing** the Web.

- URLs

  A **URL**, which stands for **Uniform Resource Locator**, is the address of a Web page. When you type a URL into a browser, the browser looks all over the Web to find the page at the address you typed. The URL of a page on the Library of Congress Web site is shown in Figure A-2. URLs are made up of the following components:
  - A **protocol** is an agreed-upon standard, and **HTTP**, which stands for **Hypertext Transfer Protocol**, is the protocol that computers on the Web use to communicate with each other. To identify a file as a page residing on the Web, the URL begins with *http* followed by a colon and two forward slashes (*http://*).
  - The next part of a URL is the **domain name** which identifies the Web server on which the Web site is stored. It consists of the name of the Web server and a top-level domain. The **top-level domain** (**TLD**) is a two- or three-letter identifier that indicates the type of Web site or company behind the Web site; for example, the *com* top-level domain usually identifies a company that operates for profit, and the *gov* top-level domain is reserved for U. S. government agencies and departments. Some top-level domains identify the country where the site or institution is located, such as *uk* for Great Britain Web sites and *de* for German Web sites. Table A-1 lists common top-level domains. The domain name often begins with the letters *www*, signifying that the location is part of the World Wide Web.
  - The last part of a URL is the **path**, which specifies the exact location and filename of the Web page on the Web server. Folder names in the path are separated by forward slashes and the filename of the current Web page follows the last slash. The URL in Figure A-2 describes a Web page stored as a file named *index.html* in the hierarchy of folders *folklife/states* stored on the Web server (domain) named *loc.gov*.

- Searching the Internet

  You can search for Web pages that contain specific information by using a search provider. A **search provider**, also called a **search engine**, is a Web site that retrieves the URLs of Web pages that contain words or phrases, called **keywords**, that you type.

FIGURE A-1: Web page containing text and graphics

URL

Graphics

Text

FIGURE A-2: Anatomy of a URL

http://www.loc.gov/folklife/states/index.html

Protocol   Domain name   Path   Filename

TABLE A-1: Examples of common top-level domains (TLDs)

TLD	intended use
.com	Commercial (for profit) companies
.net	Network organizations (computer services that connect remote computers)
.org	Nonprofit organizations
.edu	Exclusively for educational institutions of higher learning
.gov	Exclusively for U.S. government agencies, departments, and institutions
.biz	Businesses
.info	Information service providers
.name	Individuals
.pro	Exclusively for accountants, lawyers, and physicians
.uk	Web sites in United Kingdom
.ca	Web sites in Canada
.de	Web sites in Germany
.au	Web sites in Australia
.cn	Web sites in China

Internet

Starting Windows Internet Explorer 8

To begin using Internet Explorer (sometimes abbreviated as **IE**), you simply click its name on the Start menu. The exact location and name of the menu item might vary on different computers. ▓▓▓▓▓ The first thing you need to explain to the staff from Sheehan Tours is how to start Internet Explorer.

STEPS

TROUBLE
If you do not see Internet Explorer on your Start menu, point to All Programs on the Start menu, then look for it on the All Programs submenu.

1. **Click the Start button 🕮, then locate Internet Explorer on the Start menu**
   Figure A-3 shows Internet Explorer on the Start menu and on the Quick Launch toolbar.

2. **Click Internet Explorer on the Start menu**
   Internet Explorer starts and a Web page appears, or **loads**, in the program window. When a Web page loads into your browser, it communicates with the Web server and downloads a copy of the Web page from the server to your computer.

TROUBLE
If the Set Up Windows Internet Explorer 8 wizard dialog box opens on top of the browser window, see the Clues at the bottom of this page.

3. **Click the Maximize button ▭ on the Internet Explorer title bar, if necessary**
   You've already learned that the main page around which a Web site is built is called the home page. The first page that opens when you start a browser is also called the **home page**. This type of home page is also sometimes called a **start page**. You can customize the start page to be any page on the Web. Companies often set the home page on company computers to go to the company's Web site. Figure A-4 shows the default home page for employees at Quest Specialty Travel. This is also the home page for Quest's Web site.

Starting Internet Explorer 8 for the first time

The first time you start Internet Explorer 8, the Set Up Windows Internet Explorer 8 wizard starts. (A **wizard** is a series of dialog boxes that takes you step by step through a process.) The first dialog box in the wizard welcomes you to the program and describes new features. Click Next to proceed to the second dialog box, in which you can choose whether to turn on the Suggested Sites feature. The Suggested Sites feature analyzes your browsing history (Web sites you have visited previously) and suggests Web sites that you might be interested in viewing when you click the Suggested Sites button in the Favorites bar. Click the option you prefer (you can change this later), and then click Next to display the Choose your settings dialog box. Here you can choose to use express settings or customize the rest of the settings. The express settings set Live Search as the search provider (or, if Internet Explorer 8 was installed as an update to Internet Explorer 7, the selected search provider used in Internet Explorer 7), install four accelerators, enable the SmartScreen Filter, and set the Compatibility Feature to use updates. You will learn about all of these features in this book. The easiest choice is to click the Use express settings option button, and then click Finish to close the wizard.

FIGURE A-3: Internet Explorer on the Start menu and Quick Launch toolbar

Internet Explorer on the Start menu

Internet Explorer on the Quick Launch toolbar (might not appear on your screen)

Start button

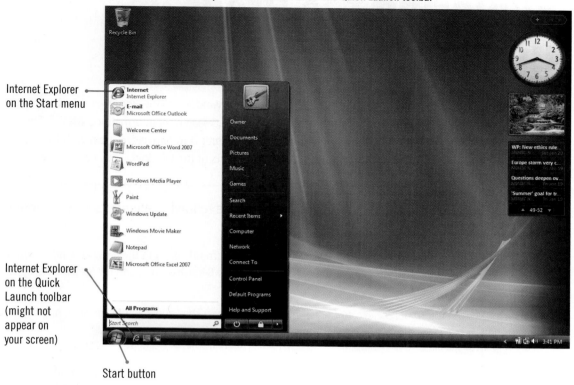

FIGURE A-4: Default start page for employees at Quest Specialty Travel

Exploring the Program Window

When you start Internet Explorer, the Internet Explorer program window, or the **browser window**, opens. The screen elements in this window enable you to view, enter, and search for information. ████ The next step in teaching the Boston employees how to use Internet Explorer is to familiarize them with the Internet Explorer program window. You identify and label the various parts of the window for the employees.

DETAILS

Use Figure A-5 as a guide to help you locate each of the following elements on your screen:

- **Address bar**

  The **Address bar** shows the complete URL of the Web page currently open in the browser window. On the right end of the Address bar the Compatibility View button, the Refresh button, and the Stop button appear.

- **Navigation buttons**

  The navigation buttons are located to the left of the Address bar. They allow you to move among the Web pages you have viewed during the current browsing session.

- **Search box**

  You can search for Web pages all over the WWW using your default search provider by typing keywords in the **Search box**, and then clicking the Search button [🔍]. You can click the Search button list arrow [▼] to access commands for managing your search providers.

- **Favorites bar**

  The **Favorites bar** contains buttons you add that give you quick access to Web sites you visit often. It also contains the Suggested Sites button, which, if this feature is turned on, you can click to see a list of five Web sites that are similar to the Web site you are viewing. Finally, the Get More Add-ons buttons in the Favorites bar displays a list of add-on programs you can add to Internet Explorer.

- **Tab row**

  Pages currently open in the browser window appear on **tabs** in the tab row. The small tab to the right of the open tabs is the **New Tab button**. When you click it, a new tabbed page opens in the browser window.

- **Command bar**

  The **Command bar** is located on the right side of the window opposite the tab row. It contains buttons that you can click to execute common commands while working in the browser. The buttons on the Command bar are described in Table A-2.

- **Browser window**

  The **browser window** is the area in which the Web page appears.

- **Status bar**

  The **status bar**, located at the bottom of the program window, displays information about the current operation; for example, when a Web page is loading, information about the status of the process appears on the left side of the status bar.

- **InPrivate status indicator**

  The **InPrivate status indicator** [🔒] lets you know whether the InPrivate feature is blocking the Web page from sending information back to the Web site owners about your browsing habits.

- **Change zoom level button**

  The **Change zoom level button** [🔍 100% ▼] on the right end of the status bar allows you to change the size of the content of Web pages displayed in the window.

FIGURE A-5: Elements of the Internet Explorer window

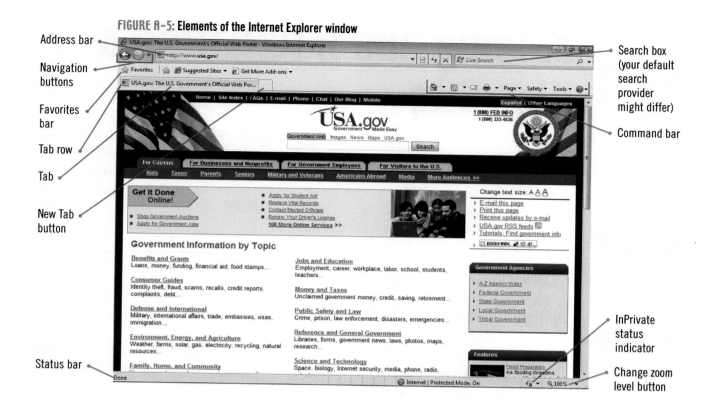

Address bar
Navigation buttons
Favorites bar
Tab row
Tab
New Tab button
Status bar

Search box (your default search provider might differ)
Command bar
InPrivate status indicator
Change zoom level button

TABLE A-2: Command bar buttons

button	name	description
	Home	Displays your home (start) page
	Feeds	Allows you to subscribe to stories that are frequently updated from that Web site
	Web Slices	Appears in place of the Feeds button only on Web pages that contain Web slices, which are portions of the Web page that are frequently updated
	Read Mail	Starts the default e-mail program
	Print	Prints the current Web page
Page ▾	Page	Opens a menu of commands for working with the open Web page
Safety ▾	Safety	Opens a menu of commands for customizing safety and privacy settings
Tools ▾	Tools	Opens a menu of commands for customizing Internet Explorer
▾	Help	Opens a menu of commands for accessing the Windows Help and Support system

Changing the start page

You can change the start page in Internet Explorer. (If you are working in a lab, this feature might be disabled. Check with your instructor.) To do this, click the Home button list arrow 🏠 ▾ on the Command bar. The first item in the menu that opens is the current start page. To change the start page to the Web page currently displayed in the browser window, click Add or Change Home Page on the menu. In the Add or Change Home Page dialog box, you can choose to use the currently displayed page as your start page; to have the current start page open in one tab and the Web page you are currently viewing open in a second tab so that you have more than one Web page open as start pages; or, if you have more than one tab open, all of the current tabs set as the home page. To set the home page so a blank page appears, click 🏠 ▾, point to Remove on the menu, click Remove All, then, in the Delete Home Page dialog box that opens, click Yes.

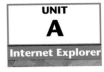

Finding and Navigating a Web Site

To display a specific Web page in the browser window, you type its URL in the Address bar. To display the home page of a Web site, you type the domain name. After a Web page is loaded, you can jump to other Web pages by clicking links. A **link** is text or a graphic formatted so that when you click it, another Web page loads in the browser window, you jump to another location on the same Web page, or you open a document stored on your computer or on a Web server. ▰▰▰▰ The first thing you want to teach the employees is how to go directly to specific Web pages.

STEPS

1. **Click anywhere in the Address bar**

   The current URL becomes highlighted in the Address text box. As with any selected text in a Windows program, you can simply type to replace all of the selected text with the text you type.

QUICK TIP

Click the Refresh button 🔄 to reload the current page, and click the Stop button ✕ to stop the page from loading.

2. **Type questspecialtytravel.com**

   The selected URL is replaced by the new URL you typed. Note that the Refresh button 🔄 changes to the Go button ➡ as soon as you start typing.

3. **Click the Go button ➡ at the right end of the Address bar**

   The URL changes to include the protocol *http://* at the beginning of the text you typed, and the Web page loads in the browser window. As the new page loads, the left end of the status bar displays information about the status of the current operation. Near the center of the status bar is the **progress bar**, which fills with green to show the status of the loading Web page, and then disappears when the Web page has finished loading. The home page for Quest Specialty Travel appears in your browser window. See Figure A-6. The page title appears in the browser window title bar and on the tab. In the Address bar, the domain name appears in dark text, and the rest of the URL is in lighter text. This is to help you quickly identify the Web site on which the page is stored.

QUICK TIP

Sometimes, text links are formatted in a different color or are underlined, but usually you cannot determine if a graphic is a link until you point to it to see if the pointer changes shape.

4. **Move the pointer over the text and graphics on the page**

   The pointer changes to 🖑 when it passes over a link.

5. **Point to the About Us link**

   The text changes color because it is a link and the URL of the link you point to appears in the status bar. See Figure A-7.

6. **Click the About Us link**

   The About Us page loads in the browser window.

7. **Click in the Address bar, then press [→]**

   The blinking insertion point appears at the end of the URL and the URL is no longer selected. You can modify the current URL rather than type a new URL to open a new Web page.

QUICK TIP

Right-click a blank area of the bar below the Address bar, point to Customize, then click Show Stop and Refresh Buttons before Address Bar to move the Stop and Refresh buttons position.

8. **Press [←] five times to position the blinking insertion point to the right of *about*, press [Backspace] five times to delete *about*, type destinations, then press [Enter]**

   Pressing [Enter] is an alternative to clicking the Go button on the Address bar. The Destinations page on the Quest Web site loads.

9. **Click the Home button 🏠 on the Command bar to return to your start page**

   Clicking the Home button loads your start page.

FIGURE A-6: Home page of Quest Specialty Travel

Web page title

Domain name

Refresh button changes to the Go button when you start typing a new URL

Compatibility View button

FIGURE A-7: Pointing to a link

Home button

Pointer positioned over a link

URL of link being pointed to

Using Compatibility View

In order for Web pages to display properly in Internet Explorer 8 and to take advantage of the new features in Internet Explorer 8, Web site designers must upgrade the content on their Web pages to be in compliance with the latest Web standards. As you surf the Web, you might encounter Web pages that are not yet upgraded. If you load a page in the browser window that is not compatible with the new standards, you can switch to **Compatibility view** by clicking the Compatibility View button ⊠ that appears on the Address bar.

Click this button to have Internet Explorer 8 display the Web page as it appears in older browsers. You can also turn this feature on permanently by clicking the Tools button on the Command bar, and then clicking Compatibility View Settings to open the Compatibility View Settings dialog box. Click the Display all websites in Compatibility View check box to select this option, ensuring that Web sites that are not yet upgraded to the new Web standards display correctly.

Navigating to Previously Visited Web Pages

As you navigate among Web pages, Internet Explorer maintains a **history**, a list of the pages you opened and the order in which you viewed them. You can use the navigation buttons next to the Address bar to move back and forward among the pages you viewed during your current Internet Explorer session. In addition, if you start to type the address of a Web site you have visited before in the Address bar, the **AutoComplete** feature opens a list with all of the URLs containing the letters you type. You can then select one of these URLs from the list. ▰▱▱ Now that the employees have visited a few Web sites, you teach them how to use the AutoComplete feature and how to move back and forward among the sites in the history list.

STEPS

1. Click in the Address bar, then type q

The URLs of Web pages previously visited whose domain names include the letter *q* appear in a drop-down list below the Address bar. See Figure A-8. The two pages on questspecialtytravel.com that you entered in the Address bar in the previous lesson are in the list. In each URL in the list, the text that you just typed in the Address bar (the letter *q*) appears in blue. You might also see sections in the list labeled History and Favorites below the URLs you recently typed listing Web pages from your history or Favorites list (a list of saved Web pages) that contain the letter *q* in the URL, the Web page title, or other properties.

QUICK TIP
Press [Shift]+[Enter] to go to the first Web page in the drop-down list.

2. Position the pointer anywhere in the row containing the URL for the Quest Specialty Travel Destinations page in the drop-down list

A Delete button ✕ appears on the right side of the list in the first row.

3. Click the Delete button ✕

The URL for the Destinations page is deleted from the list. This is useful if you notice a mistyped URL in the list and you don't want it to appear every time you type letters contained in it.

4. Click http://questspecialtytravel.com/ in the list below the Address bar

The home page on the Quest Specialty Travel Web site loads in the browser window.

5. Click the Back button ⬅ to the left of the Address bar

The previously viewed page, your start page in this case, appears in the browser window. After you use the Back button to return to an earlier page, the Forward button becomes available and appears in color.

6. Click the Forward button ➡ to the left of the Address bar

The Quest home page loads again. Notice that now the Forward button is unavailable (dimmed) because there are no more pages that you viewed after the current page in the history list. To display a list of the 10 most recently viewed pages, you can click the Recent Pages list arrow.

7. Click the Recent Pages list arrow ▾ to the left of the Address bar

A list of recently viewed pages appears.

8. Click Quest Specialty Travel :: Destinations in the list

The Destinations page on the Quest Web site loads in the browser window.

QUICK TIP
The screen shown in Figure A-9 reflects a browser with no history other than the steps taken in this unit.

9. Click the Address bar list arrow ▾

A drop-down list appears containing three sections: recently typed URLs, History, and Favorites. See Figure A-9. The Web pages listed in the History and Favorites section have URLs, Web page titles, or other properties that have something in common with the currently displayed Web page.

10. Press [Esc] to close the list without selecting anything

FIGURE A-8: Drop-down list of previously visited Web pages with *q* in the URL

Back button

Forward button
(unavailable)

Recent Pages
list arrow

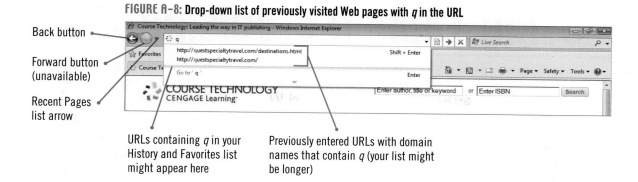

URLs containing *q* in your
History and Favorites list
might appear here

Previously entered URLs with domain
names that contain *q* (your list might
be longer)

FIGURE A-9: Address bar drop-down list

Suggestions
from History

Suggestions from
Favorites list

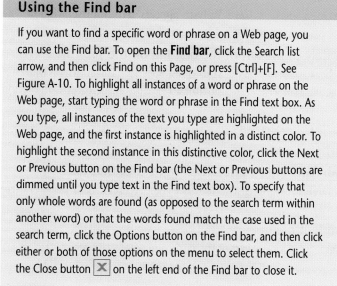

Address bar list arrow

Click to display
additional
items in History

Using the Find bar

If you want to find a specific word or phrase on a Web page, you
can use the Find bar. To open the **Find bar**, click the Search list
arrow, and then click Find on this Page, or press [Ctrl]+[F]. See
Figure A-10. To highlight all instances of a word or phrase on the
Web page, start typing the word or phrase in the Find text box. As
you type, all instances of the text you type are highlighted on the
Web page, and the first instance is highlighted in a distinct color. To
highlight the second instance in this distinctive color, click the Next
or Previous button on the Find bar (the Next or Previous buttons are
dimmed until you type text in the Find text box). To specify that
only whole words are found (as opposed to the search term within
another word) or that the words found match the case used in the
search term, click the Options button on the Find bar, and then click
either or both of those options on the menu to select them. Click
the Close button ☒ on the left end of the Find bar to close it.

FIGURE A-10: Find bar

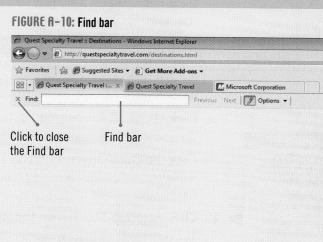

Click to close
the Find bar

Find bar

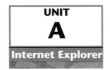
Using Tabbed Browsing

Tabbed browsing allows you to open multiple Web pages in the browser window. The title of the Web page appears on the tab itself, and the Web page appears in the window below the tab. To open a new Web page without closing the current page, you open a new tab and load the new Web page in that tab. The tab that is on top is called the **active tab**. When you open multiple tabs, they are automatically sorted into **tab groups**, collections of related tabs. The tabs in a tab group all appear in the same color so that you can easily see which tabs are related to each other. You decide to explain tabbed browsing next so that the employees can jump quickly from one Web page to another.

STEPS

1. **Point to the New Tab button to the right of the Quest Specialty Travel :: Destinations tab so that the New Tab icon appears on it, then click**

   A new tab opens on top of the Destinations page and the New Tab button shifts to the right. The new tab contains links for reopening closed tabs and the previous browsing session, and for accessing new features in Internet Explorer 8. The Quick Tabs button and the Tab List arrow appear to the left of the first tab. See Figure A-11. Notice the text in the Address bar is selected.

TROUBLE

If a dialog box opens asking if you want to install Microsoft Silverlight, click No thanks.

2. **Type microsoft.com, then click the Go button**

   The text you typed replaces the selected text in the Address bar, and the home page on the Microsoft Web site opens in the new tab.

3. **Click the Quest Specialty Travel :: Destinations tab**

   The Destinations page on the Quest Web site becomes the active tab.

4. **Right-click the Quest logo in the upper left of the Web page, then click Open Link in New Tab on the shortcut menu**

   The Quest logo is a link to the Quest Specialty Travel home page. A new tab opens behind the current tab—that is, between the Destinations and the Microsoft page—and the Quest home page loads in that tab. Because you opened the new tab by right-clicking a link, the tabs for the two Quest pages are colored green to indicate that they belong to the same tab group.

5. **Right-click the About Us link, and then click Open Link in New Tab**

   A third Quest Specialty Travel tab opens. As you add tabs, the tabs shrink and you can't see the complete page name on each tab.

QUICK TIP

You can change the tab order by dragging a tab left or right to a new position on the Tab row.

6. **Point to the leftmost Quest tab to see a ScreenTip that identifies it as the Destinations page, then click the middle Quest tab**

   The tab displaying the home page for the Quest Specialty Travel Web site appears in the browser window. The other Quest Specialty Travel pages and the Microsoft page are hidden behind the current Web page.

7. **Click the Tab List arrow immediately to the left of the first tab on the Tab row**

   A list of currently open tabs appears. A check mark appears next to Quest Specialty Travel, which indicates that this is the page displayed on the active tab. The faint horizontal line above Microsoft Corporation separates the two tab groups.

8. **Click Microsoft Corporation in the list**

   The Microsoft Corporation tab becomes the active tab.

9. **Click the Quest Specialty Travel tab (the middle one), then right-click that tab**

   A shortcut menu opens containing commands for working with tabs. See Table A-3 for a description of these commands.

QUICK TIP

Click the Quick Tabs button to the left of the first tab to display thumbnail images depicting each of the open tabs in the window.

10. **Click Ungroup This Tab on the shortcut menu**

    The tab is recolored white to indicate that it is no longer part of the tab group whose tabs are colored green, and it is shifted to the right so it is no longer located in the middle of the tab group. See Figure A-12.

FIGURE A-11: New tab open

Quick Tabs button

Tab list arrow

One page listed in the Reopen closed tabs list (there might be more or nothing listed on your screen)

Click to reopen the last browsing session (will not appear on your screen if this is your first browsing session)

New Tab button

New tab

Links to new features in Internet Explorer 8

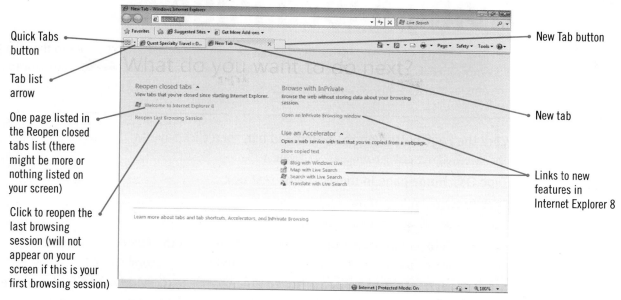

FIGURE A-12: Tab row after ungrouping a tab

Tab group

Ungrouped tab

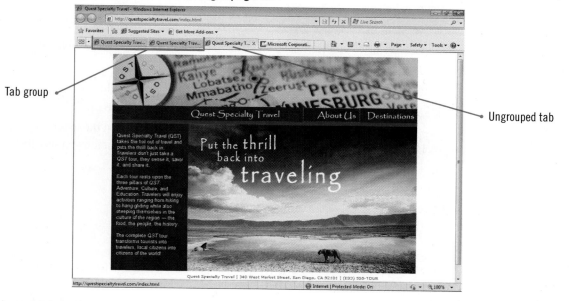

TABLE A-3: Commands on tab shortcut menu

command	description
Close Tab	Closes the current tab
Close This Tab Group	Closes all tabs in the current tab group
Close Other Tabs	Closes all tabs except for the current tab
Ungroup This Tab	Removes the current tab from its tab group
Refresh	Reloads the page displayed in the current tab
Refresh All	Reloads all of the pages displayed in all open tabs
New Tab	Opens a new tab
Duplicate Tab	Opens a new tab with the current page loaded in it
Reopen Closed Tab	Reopens the most recently closed tab
Recently Closed Tabs	Displays a list of recently closed tabs

Saving a Web Page

You can save a Web page to your hard disk. This can be useful if you need to refer back to the Web page and you know it changes frequently, for example a newspaper's home page.  You want to make sure the employees know how to save a Web page so that they can refer to it later.

1. **Click the Page button on the Command bar, then click Save As**
   The Save Webpage dialog box opens. See Figure A-13.

2. **Type QST Home page in the File name text box**

3. **Click Browse Folders, if necessary**
   The dialog box expands to display the Navigation pane.

4. **Click the Folders bar in the Navigation pane to expand the Folder list, if necessary**
   The list of all the folders and drives on the computer expands in the Navigation pane.

5. **Scroll down the Folders list in the Navigation pane to find the drive and folder where you store your Data Files, then click the drive and folder to open it in the window**
   See Figure A-14.

6. **Click the Save as type list arrow**
   Four options are listed on the drop-down list. These choices are described in Table A-4.

TROUBLE
> 7. **Click Web Archive, single file (*.mht)**
>   This is the default options.

TROUBLE
If filename extensions are hidden on your computer, *(*.mht)* will not be part of the Save as type name.

8. **Click Save**
   The Save As dialog box closes, and another dialog box briefly appears on the screen showing the progress of the save action. That dialog box closes, and the page is saved to the location you specified.

Sending a Web page as an e-mail message or as a link

You can send a Web page as an e-mail message. To do this, click the Page button on the Command bar, then click Send Page by E-mail. The Internet Explorer Security dialog box might open warning you that the program that you are trying to open is outside of Internet Explorer's Protected mode. Click Allow. A new e-mail message window opens with the Web page as the body of the message. Type the recipient's e-mail address in the To text box. The Subject of the message is already filled in as "Emailing:" followed by the name of the Web page. When the recipient receives and opens your message, the Web page will appear as the body of the message. To send the URL of the Web page as a link in an e-mail message, click the Page button on the Command bar, then click Send Link by E-mail. A new e-mail message window opens with the URL of the Web page in the body of the message. When the recipient opens the e-mail message, the URL will appear as a link. If you have a Windows Live account, you can click the Page button on the Command bar, then click E-mail with Windows Live to open a new tab displaying the log-in page for your Windows Live account. After logging in, a new e-mail message in Hotmail opens with a link to the current page in the body of the message.

FIGURE A-13: Save Webpage dialog box

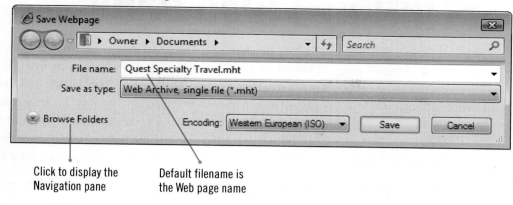

Click to display the
Navigation pane

Default filename is
the Web page name

FIGURE A-14: Save Folders list expanded in the Save Webpage dialog box

Current
folder

Navigation
pane

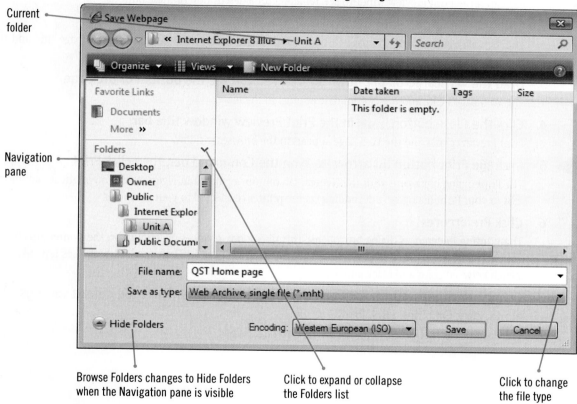

Browse Folders changes to Hide Folders
when the Navigation pane is visible

Click to expand or collapse
the Folders list

Click to change
the file type

TABLE A-4: File types available on the Save as type list

Save as type	description
Webpage, complete (*.htm;*.html)	Saves the Web page as a file and all the files associated with it, such as the graphics, styles, and so on, in a separate folder
Web Archive, single file (*.mht)	Saves the Web page as a single file
Webpage, HTML only (*.htm;*.html)	Saves only the formatted text on the page
Text File (*.txt)	Saves the unformatted text on the page

Printing a Web Page

Internet Explorer enables you to print the Web page displayed in your browser window. Printing a Web page can be useful if you find information that you'd like to review later, away from your computer. It also allows you to easily share information you find on the Web with friends and associates. **Print Preview** shows you how the current Web page will look when it is printed. Because Web pages are not designed to necessarily fit on a sheet of paper, it is always a good idea to preview one before you print it. 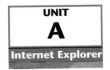 Because customers might want to bring a printed Web page to refer to when they leave the office, you next explain to the employees how to use Print Preview and how to print a Web page.

STEPS

1. **Click the Print button list arrow 🖨 ▾ on the Command bar, then click Print Preview**

   The Print Preview window opens, as shown in Figure A-15. Because Web pages are designed to be viewed online, the content does not always neatly fit onto an 8½" x 11" sheet of paper. You can adjust the content to fit on the paper or change the **orientation** (the direction of the paper) by selecting the options on the toolbar in the Print Preview window. See Table A-5 for a description of these buttons.

   QUICK TIP

   If the content appears on more than one page and you don't want it to shrink to fit on one page, you can click the Change Print Size button, and then click 100%.

2. **Click the View Full Width button 🖵 on the toolbar**

   The view changes so that the page fills the width of the screen. Notice that the Web page title and the number of pages appear in the header.

3. **Drag the vertical scroll bar down so that you can see the bottom of the page**

   The Web page's URL and the current date appears in the footer.

4. **Click the Close button ▣✕▣ in the Print Preview window title bar**

   Print Preview closes and the Web page appears in the browser window.

   QUICK TIP

   To print the page with the default settings, click the Print button on the Command bar.

5. **Click the Print button list arrow 🖨 ▾ on the Command bar, then click Print**

   The Print dialog box opens with the General tab on top, as shown in Figure A-16. You might see additional tabs in your Print dialog box, depending on the printer connected to your computer.

6. **Click Preferences**

   The Printing Preferences dialog box opens. This dialog box changes depending on the printer attached to your computer. Usually, you can choose to print the Web page in Draft mode, which uses less ink, or to switch between color and black and white.

7. **Change printing settings as directed by your instructor or leave the default settings alone, click OK, then click Print**

   The Print dialog box closes, and the current Web page prints.

Printing a graphic or text on a Web page

Sometimes you want to print only an image or specific text on a Web page, not the entire page. You can do this easily. To print a graphic on a Web page, right-click the graphic, then click Print Picture on the shortcut menu. To print specific text, position the pointer at the beginning of the text you want to print so that the pointer changes to I. Press and hold the left mouse button, drag over the text you want to print to select it, and then release the mouse button. Right-click the selected text, and then click Print to open the Print dialog box. In the Page Range section, click the Selection option button, and then click Print.

FIGURE A-15: Print Preview window

Toolbar

View Full Width button

View Full Page button

Web page title

URL of current Web page

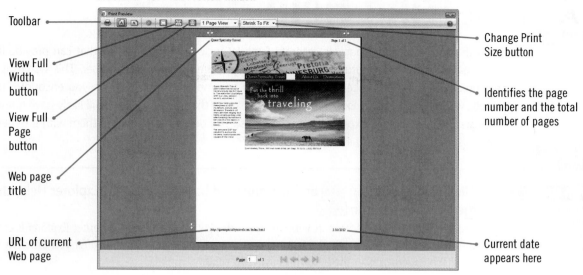

Change Print Size button

Identifies the page number and the total number of pages

Current date appears here

FIGURE A-16: Print dialog box

Your list of printers might differ

Options for changing the number of pages printed

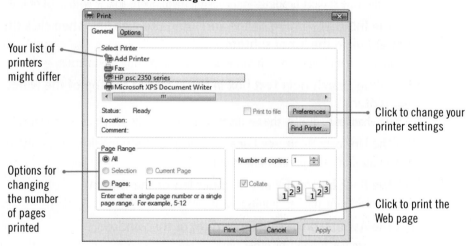

Click to change your printer settings

Click to print the Web page

TABLE A-5: Buttons on the toolbar in Print Preview

button	name	description
	Print Document	Prints the current Web page
	Portrait	Displays the page in Portrait view (the page is taller than it is wide)
	Landscape	Displays the page in Landscape view (the page is wider than it is tall)
	Page Setup	Opens the Page Setup dialog box; many options in this dialog box appear on the toolbar in the Print Preview window
	Turn headers and footers on or off	Toggles the headers and footers on or off
	View Full Width	Changes the view so that the page fills the width of the screen
	View Full Page	Changes the view so the length of the page is visible on the screen
1 Page View ▼	Show multiple pages	Changes the view to view multiple pages at a time
Shrink To Fit ▼	Change Print Size	Changes the zoom settings for printing the page
	Help	Opens the Windows Help and How-to page on Microsoft.com in a new window

Internet

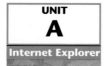

Getting Help

As with most Windows programs, Internet Explorer includes a Help system that can provide information and instructions on the features and commands you are using in the browser. This system is a valuable resource when you are uncertain about how to accomplish a task or when you encounter unexpected results while using Internet Explorer. ▧▦▦▦ You know that the employees will likely have questions when they start to use Internet Explorer on their own, so you decide to familiarize them with Internet Explorer's Help system.

STEPS

QUICK TIP

You can also press [F1] to open the Help and Support window.

1. **Click the Help button 🔵▾ on the Command bar, click Internet Explorer Help, then click the Maximize button 🔲**

   The Windows Help and Support window opens displaying the page for Internet Explorer 8 at a glance, as shown in Figure A-17. The buttons at the upper right of the Help window offer you different ways to use Help. Table A-6 describes the buttons in the Help window.

2. **Click the Browse Help button 🔳 at the upper right of the window**

   The main contents page for help with Internet Explorer opens with a list of links. The links with the book next to them are subject headings and clicking them opens a page with a list of links about that subject.

3. **Click the Internet – going online and using the web link, then click the Exploring the Internet link in the list of subtopics**

   The window changes to display information about exploring the Internet, as shown in Figure A-18.

4. **Click in the Search Help text box in the center at the top of the window, type url, then press [Enter]**

   The page changes to display the results that best match the search term you typed.

5. **Click the Uniform Resource Locator (URL) (definition) link in the list of topics**

   The definition of URL appears in the window.

6. **Click the Back button ◀ at the upper left of the window**

   The page displaying the best results appears again.

7. **Click the Ask button at the upper right of the window**

   The Get customer support or other types of help page opens. The links on this page bring you to other support options from a friend, from Microsoft, or from your computer's manufacturer.

8. **Click the Close button ❎ in the upper-right corner of the Help window to close it**

   The Help window on top of the Internet Explorer browser window closes.

FIGURE A-17: Windows Help and Support window displaying information about Internet Explorer 8

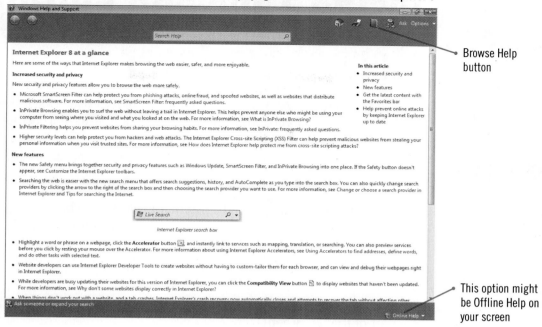

Browse Help button

This option might be Offline Help on your screen

FIGURE A-18: Exploring the Internet page in Windows Help and Support window

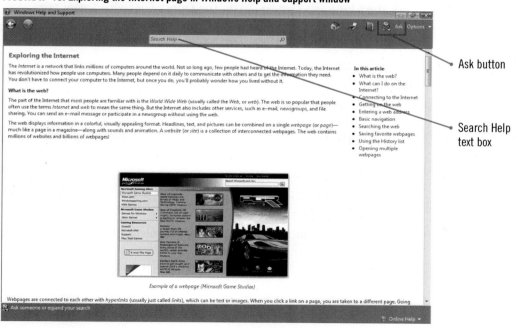

Ask button

Search Help text box

TABLE A-6: Descriptions of the Help options

button	name	description
	Help and Support home	Jumps to the home page of Windows Help and Support
	Print	Prints the current Help topic
	Browse Help	Opens a list of subject headings for help on Internet Explorer
	Ask	Opens a window listing additional ways and links for getting help and support
	Options	Opens a menu of commands for working with Help

Closing Tabs and Exiting Internet Explorer

In many other Windows programs, you need to save documents before exiting. However, a Web browser simply displays existing documents and allows the user to interact with them; it does not make changes to Web pages themselves. Therefore, you can close Internet Explorer at any time without losing data. ▰▰▰▰ You need to teach the employees how to close tabs and exit the browser when they have finished.

STEPS

1. **Click the Close button** ❌ **on the Internet Explorer title bar**

   A dialog box opens warning you that you are about to close more than one tab. See Figure A-19.

2. **Click the Close button** ❌ **on the dialog box title bar**

3. **Point to the Close Tab button** ❌ **on the Quest Specialty Travel tab (the Quest tab that is not part of the tab group)**

   The Close Tab button changes to ❌. See Figure A-20.

4. **Click the Close Tab button** ❌ **on the Quest Specialty Travel tab**

   The Quest tab closes and the Microsoft home page becomes the active tab. You can reopen tabs you close.

5. **Right-click the Microsoft Corporation tab, point to Recently Closed Tabs, and then click Quest Specialty Travel**

   The Quest Specialty Travel home page opens again.

6. **Right-click the Microsoft Corporation tab, then click Close Other Tabs on the shortcut menu**

   All of the tabs except the current tab close.

7. **Click** ❌ **on the Internet Explorer title bar**

   The Internet Explorer program window closes, and you return to the Windows desktop.

Changing tab settings

You can change the default behavior for tabs. Click the Tools button on the Command bar, then click Internet Options to open the Internet Options dialog box with the General tab on top. Click Settings in the Tabs section of the dialog box to open the Tabbed Browsing Settings dialog box. Deselecting the first option disables tabs completely. The rest of the check boxes allow you to control the behavior of tabs, including whether to use tab groups. You can click the When a new tab is opened, open list arrow to choose the tab that opens when a new tab is created. The option buttons in the middle of the dialog box control the behavior of pop-ups, which are new browser windows that a Web site tries to open on your computer. Finally, the option buttons at the bottom of the dialog box control how links from other programs that open Web pages appear.

FIGURE A-19: Dialog box warning that multiple tabs will be closed

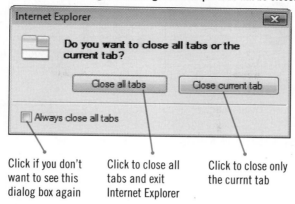

Click if you don't want to see this dialog box again

Click to close all tabs and exit Internet Explorer

Click to close only the currnt tab

FIGURE A-20: Using the Close Tab button

Close Tab button

Internet

Practice

If you have a SAM user profile, you may have access to hands-on instruction, practice, and assessment of the skills covered in this unit. Log in to your SAM account (http://sam2007.course.com/) to launch any assigned training activities or exams that relate to the skills covered in this unit.

▼ CONCEPTS REVIEW

Label each component of the Internet Explorer program window shown in Figure A-21.

FIGURE A-21

Match each term with the statement that best describes it.

10. URL
11. home page
12. Web browser
13. Web server
14. Web site
15. Web page
16. domain name

a. A computer or a network of computers that stores Web pages and makes them available on the Web

b. A collection of related Web pages stored on a Web server

c. The first page that opens when you start a browser or the main page around which the Web site is built

d. Software that allows you to navigate to, open, view, and interact with files on the Web

e. A specially formatted file designed for use on the Web

f. The address of a Web page

g. Identifies the Web server on which the Web site is stored; it consists of a name identifying the Web server and a top-level domain

Select the best answer from the list of choices.

17. Which of the following is the protocol that all computers on the Web use to communicate with each other?

   a. HTTP   **c.** TLD

   b. URL   **d.** .com

18. Which of the following is a two- or three-letter identifier that identifies the type of Web site or company behind the Web site?

   a. Domain name   **c.** Path

   b. Top-level domain   **d.** Protocol

19. A subset of the Internet is:

   a. a Web page   **c.** a URL

   b. the World Wide Web   **d.** the protocol

20. To go directly to a Web site, where do you type the URL before clicking the Go button?

   a. Tab   **c.** Home page

   b. Address bar   **d.** Title bar

21. To go to the Web page you viewed immediately prior to the current Web page, which button do you click?

   a. History   **c.** Back

   b. Refresh   **d.** Forward

22. To quickly jump to another Web page, another location on the same Web page, or to another document, you click a:

   a. link   **c.** Back button

   b. tab   **d.** URL

23. Which of the following is the list of the pages you opened in the order you viewed them?

   a. History list   **c.** Tab list

   b. Address list   **d.** Back list

24. To see what a Web page will look like when it is printed, switch to:

   a. Print Preview   **c.** Full Width view

   b. Normal view   **d.** Web page view

25. To see multiple pages in the browser window, you can open additional:

   a. windows   **c.** browsers

   b. tabs   **d.** panes

26. Another term for browsing the Web is:

   a. naming   **c.** texting

   b. webbing   **d.** surfing

27. To save a complete Web page, including graphics, as a single file, you choose which file type?

   a. Webpage complete   **c.** Webpage, HTML only

   b. Web Archive, single file   **d.** Text File

▼ SKILLS REVIEW

1. **Understand Web browsing.**
   a. Explain the difference between the Internet and the World Wide Web.
   b. Explain what a Web page, Web site, and Web server are.
   c. Describe what a Web browser is and explain what you use it to do.
   d. Explain what a URL is, then describe its three parts.
   e. Explain what a protocol is and give the name of the protocol that a computer uses to communicate on the Web.

2. **Start Windows Internet Explorer 8 and explore the program window.**
   a. Start Internet Explorer.
   b. Identify as many elements in the program window as you can.
   c. Point to each button on the Command bar to see its name.

3. **Find and navigate a Web site.**
   a. Click in the Address bar.
   b. Type **www.ap.org**, then click the Go button to open the home page of the Associated Press.
   c. Identify the domain name where the Web page is stored by looking at the dark text in the Address bar.
   d. Move the pointer over the page to identify links.
   e. Look at the status bar when you point to the links, then click any link on the page whose URL starts with "http://www.ap.org".
   f. Delete all of the text in the URL in the Address bar after *ap.org*, then press [Enter] to return to the AP home page.
   g. Use the Home button to return to the browser's home page.

4. **Navigate to previously visited Web pages.**
   a. Click in the Address bar, then type **ap**.
   b. Click **www.ap.org** in the drop-down list below the Address bar.
   c. Click the Back button to return to the home page.
   d. Click the Forward button to return to the AP home page.
   e. Open the Recent Pages list, then click the URL for the link you clicked when you originally visited the AP home page (in Skills Review 3e).
   f. Open the Address bar drop-down list, then delete the URL for the AP home page.

5. **Use tabbed browsing.**
   a. Open a new tab.
   b. In the new tab, go to the home page for *The New York Times* at **www.nytimes.com**.
   c. Open any link on the page in a new tab.
   d. Identify the tabs in the tab group.
   e. Use the Tab List to switch to the new page you opened in step c.
   f. Ungroup the tab containing the new page you opened.
   g. Click the tab for the home page on *The New York Times'* site.

6. **Save a Web page.**
   a. Click the Page button on the Command bar, then click Save As.
   b. Type **NYTimes home page** as the new filename.
   c. Use the Folders list to navigate to the drive and folder where you are storing your Data Files.
   d. Make sure the page will be saved as a Web Archive, single file.
   e. Click Save.

▼ SKILLS REVIEW (CONTINUED)

7. **Print a Web page.**
   a. Open Print Preview.
   b. Zoom in on the page so the width of the page fills the width of the screen.
   c. Switch the view back to Full Page view.
   d. Close the Print Preview window, then open the Print dialog box.
   e. Click the Pages option button, then type **1** in the Pages text box, if necessary.
   f. Print the Web page.

8. **Get help.**
   a. Open the Windows Help and Support window.
   b. Click the Browse Help button at the top of the dialog box, click the Internet – going online and using the web link, and then click the Find your computer's IP address link. Read the information in the window, clicking any links as needed to read more.
   c. Use the Ask button at the top of the dialog box to examine other methods of getting help and support.
   d. Click in the Search Help text box, type **save Web page**, press [Enter], then click the Save a webpage as a file link.
   e. Close the Help window.

9. **Close tabs and exit Internet Explorer.**
   a. Make the tab containing the page on the AP Web site the active tab, then use the Close Tab button to close the AP tab.
   b. Use the tab shortcut menu to reopen the tab containing the page from the AP Web site.
   c. Use the Close Tab command on the shortcut menu to close the tab containing the page on the AP Web site, then close the Internet Explorer program window.

▼ INDEPENDENT CHALLENGE 1

You own a small cabin near a lake in New Hampshire and you want to rent it for the month of August. You decide to create flyers to advertise your cabin. Your printer recently broke, so you decide to buy a new one. You want one that will also scan photos so that you can include photos of your cabin. You are on a tight budget, so you decide to research printers from several manufacturers to find the best printer for a low price.

   a. Start Internet Explorer.
   b. Go to **www.canon.com**. Click links on the Canon Web site to find a list of their inkjet printers. (*Hint*: As you navigate links, some Web pages might open in a new browser window rather than load in the current tab.)
   c. Open a new tab, then go to **www.hp.com**. Click links on the Hewlett-Packard site to find a printer that meets your needs.
   d. Go to **www.epson.com** in a new tab, then click links to find an Epson printer that meets your needs.
   e. Decide which printer you want, and then print the product information page for that printer. Shrink the text to fit on one page, if necessary.
   f. Save the product information page for your second choice printer as a Web Archive, single file named Printer Product Page in the drive and folder where you store your Data Files.
   g. Close all open tabs and exit Internet Explorer.

▼ INDEPENDENT CHALLENGE 2

Internet Explorer 8 has many new features that were not included in previous versions of the program. You decide to research some of these new features.

    a. Start Internet Explorer.

    b. Go to **www.microsoft.com**.

    c. Click in the Search box on the page, type **Internet Explorer 8**, then press [Enter].

    d. Scroll down the list of search results, then click the link for the Internet Explorer 8 home page.

    e. Explore the Internet Explorer 8 home page. When you find a link that interests you, open it in a new tab. Open at least three additional pages in new tabs.

    f. Ungroup the Internet Explorer 8 home page from the rest of the tabs.

    g. Print the page on one of the tabs. Shrink the text to fit on one page, if necessary.

    h. Save the same page you printed as a Text File named **IE8 Features** to the drive and folder where you store your Data Files.

    i. Close all open tabs and exit Internet Explorer.

▼ INDEPENDENT CHALLENGE 3

You are teaching a course on British government. You're preparing to assign a research project to your students to discuss and compare the main bodies of British government—the Cabinet, the House of Commons, and the House of Lords. You want to require your students to do some of their research on the Internet, so you decide to investigate a couple of URLs for British government sites to make sure this is a reasonable expectation.

    a. Start Internet Explorer.

    b. Go to **www.number-10.gov.uk**.

    c. Open any link in a new tab, and then ungroup the tabs.

    d. In a new tab, go to **www.parliament.uk**.

Advanced Challenge Exercise

    ■ Click the Change Zoom Level button on the right end of the status bar, then click it again.

    ■ Click the Change Zoom Level button arrow, then click 100% on the menu.

    ■ Click the Page button on the Command bar, point to Text Size, then click Largest.

    ■ Use the Text Size command on the Page button menu to change the Text Size to Smallest, and then return to Medium.

    e. Save each open page as a Web Archive, single file to the drive and folder where you store your Data Files. Name the first one **UK Government 1**, the second **UK Government 2**, and the third **UK Government 3**.

    f. Print the home page of each Web site. Shrink the text to fit on one page, if necessary.

    g. Close all open tabs and exit Internet Explorer.

▼ REAL LIFE INDEPENDENT CHALLENGE

At some point, you will need to create or update a résumé that you can send to potential employers when you are searching for a new job. It is a good idea to look at a few example résumés to help you as you create your own.

    a. Start Internet Explorer.

    b. Go to **www.google.com**.

    c. Click in the Search text box, type **resume examples**, then click Google Search. A list of Web pages that contain the keywords you searched for opens. The results are links to the Web page listed.

    d. Examine the list of search results. Read the page descriptions under each link to find pages that look like they might have the information you want.

    e. Open at least four pages in new tabs that look like they might have example résumés that you can look at.

Advanced Challenge Exercise

    ■ Make the most promising page the active tab, click the Page button on the Command bar, then click Send Page by E-mail.

    ■ In the Internet Explorer Security dialog box that opens, click Allow.

    ■ In the new e-mail message window that opens, type your e-mail address in the To text box, then click the Send (or something similar) button to send the Web page as the body of an e-mail message to yourself.

    f. Examine the pages that you opened. From one of the sites, open a page that contains a sample résumé, then print that résumé.

    g. Save one of the résumés as a Webpage, complete file named **Sample Resume** to the drive and folder where you store your Data Files.

    h. Close all open tabs and exit Internet Explorer.

▼ VISUAL WORKSHOP

Use the skills you learned in this lesson to open the Web pages in tabs as shown in Figure A-22. The URLs for the pages shown in the first three tabs are:

www.course.com
www.microsoft.com
www.nasa.gov

Open the About NASA page on the NASA site in a fourth tab that is grouped with the NASA home page. (The color of the tab group on your screen might differ from the one shown in Figure A-22.) Print a copy of the About NASA page. Note that because most Web sites are updated on a regular basis, the content and/or layout of the Web page that you print might differ from the content and layout of the page shown in Figure A-22.

FIGURE A-22

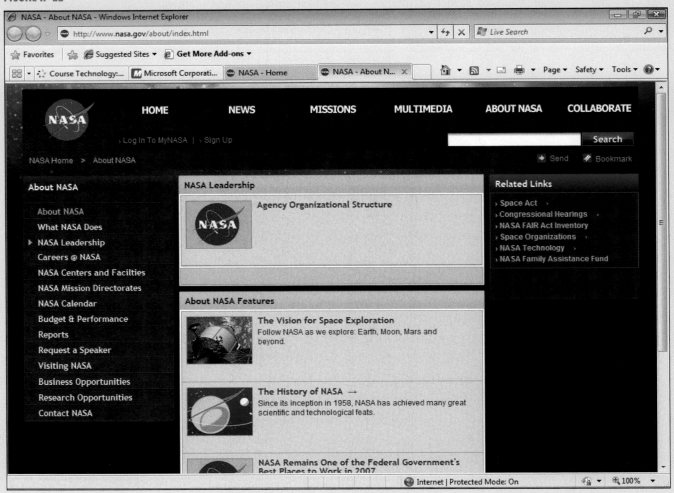

Getting the Most from Internet Explorer 8

Files You Will Need:

No Files Needed.

Now that you are familiar with the toolbars, menus, dialog boxes, and Help system of Internet Explorer, you are ready to use its more advanced features. This unit introduces you to searching the Web for information about a particular topic, saving the URL for a page so that you can easily return to it, having headlines delivered to you on a regular basis, copying and saving text and graphics from a Web page, browsing securely, and adding functionality to Internet Explorer with add-on programs.  You are confident that the Boston staff of Quest Specialty Travel is comfortable with the basics of using Internet Explorer 8. You want to teach them how to find and use specific information on the Web and to do this with a reasonable degree of confidence that they are using the Web securely. You also want to teach them about additional programs that enhance Internet Explorer 8.

OBJECTIVES

Use the Search box

Create and use favorites

Manage favorites

Explore add-ons

Use Accelerators

Use newsfeeds and Web Slices

Use the History list

Use the SmartScreen Filter

Use InPrivate Filtering and Browsing

Manage pop-ups

Check the security of a Web page

Using the Search Box

Recall from Unit A that a search provider (sometimes called a search engine) is a Web site that searches the Web for pages that contain the word (called a keyword) or phrase you type; the keyword or phrase is called the **search expression**. You can go to a search provider's Web site, or you can type a search expression in the **Search box**, sometimes called the **Instant Search box**, in the upper right of the Internet Explorer window, and then click the Search button 🔍 or press [Enter] to search the Web using your default search provider. The Web page that opens is the **search results page**; it contains links (**search results** or simply **results**) to Web pages that contain your search expression. ▅▅▅▅ You decide to demonstrate how to search the Web by searching for competing tour packages to Australia and Asia.

STEPS

QUICK TIP

The steps and figures in this book show Live Search, the default Microsoft search provider. If your default search provider is different, you should still be able to execute the steps in this lesson.

1. **Start Internet Explorer, and then maximize the program window if necessary**

   Your start page opens in the browser window.

2. **At the upper right of the Internet Explorer window, click in the Search box**

   A box appears below the Search box displaying the logos of the current search providers.

3. **Type australia**

   Search expressions are not case sensitive, so it doesn't matter whether you type "Australia" or "australia." As you type, a list of suggestions for completing the search expression appears below the search box, and the list changes to display results filtered to match the letters you are typing. Figure B-1 shows Live Search, which offers Visual Search. This means it displays images along with suggestions.

QUICK TIP

To see additional results pages, look for links to those pages, which are usually located at the bottom of the page.

4. **Press the [Spacebar], type tours, then click the Search button 🔍**

   A search results page opens listing links to Web pages that contain the words "Australia" and "tours." Figure B-2 shows the results when the default search provider is Live Search. If your default search provider is not Live Search, your search results page will look different, but it will contain the same basic elements. To open any of the Web pages found as a result of your search, click the link in the results page. Most search providers identify the number of results at the top of the page. The number you see will differ from the one in Figure B-2, but it will likely be in the millions. If your initial search produces too many results to be useful, you can narrow your search by adding additional terms to the search expression.

5. **At the top of the search results page, click in the search text box after the word "tours," press [Spacebar], type active adventure backpacking, then press [Enter]**

   The number of search results drops dramatically. You can add search providers to the Search box.

QUICK TIP

Click Find on this Page on the Search button menu to open the Find bar to search for text on the current Web page.

6. **At the upper right of the Internet Explorer window, click the Search button list arrow 🔍▾**

   A menu opens listing the current search providers as well as commands for finding and managing search providers. See Figure B-3. The default search provider is in bold and is labeled as the default.

7. **Click Find More Providers on the menu, then scroll down the page that opens**

   A Web page opens listing additional search providers that you can add. In addition to traditional search providers, such as Google and Yahoo, that search the entire Web, the list includes providers such as the New York Times and Amazon that execute your searches only on that site.

8. **Click 🔍▾, then click Manage Search Providers**

   The Manage Add-ons window opens on top of the browser window with Search Providers selected in the Add-on Types list on the left. You can click a search provider in the list and identify it as the default, remove it from the list, change the order of it in the list, and enable or disable search suggestions for that provider.

9. **Click Close at the bottom of the Manage Add-ons window to close it**

10. **Click in the Search box, then press [Delete] to clear the search expression from the Search box**

Live Search icon
(might be different
on your screen)

Search suggestions

Your home page will
be different

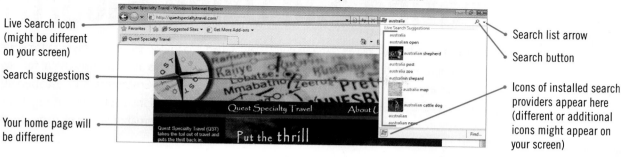

Search list arrow

Search button

Icons of installed search
providers appear here
(different or additional
icons might appear on
your screen)

FIGURE B-2: Search results for "australia tours" in Live Search

Total number of
search results
(your number
will be different)

Search
expression

Search expression
automatically
added to the
Search text box

Search
results

FIGURE B-3: Search button menu

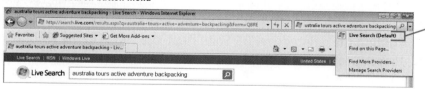

List of installed
search providers
(yours might differ
and might contain
more providers)

Creating a new search provider

You can create a search provider from almost any Web site that includes a search box. Click the Search button list arrow, then click Find More Providers to open the Search Providers Web page in the Internet Explorer 8 Add-ons Gallery. Scroll to the bottom of the page, then click the Create your own Search Provider link. Next, open a new tab in the browser window and go to the Web site you want to use. For example, if you wanted to look up definitions from the Search box, go to www.dictionary.com in the new tab. Click in the search box on the Web page, type TEST, and then click the

Search button or press [Enter]. After the search results page is loaded, click in the Address bar to select the entire URL, right-click the selected URL, then click Copy. Click the Create your own Search Provider tab, right-click in the URL text box, then click Paste to paste the copied URL in the text box. Click in the Name text box, then type a name for this search provider. Finally, click Install Search Provider. The Add Search Provider dialog box opens. Click Add to close the dialog box and add the search provider. Click the Search button list arrow to see the search provider in the list.

Internet

Creating and Using Favorites

A **favorite** is the address of a Web page that you have saved in a folder. You click a favorite to return to the Web page it points to instead of trying to remember the URL. Favorites are especially useful for pages that you find particularly significant and expect to visit repeatedly. ██████ Customers of Quest Specialty Travel who plan to travel overseas from the United States often have questions about current regulations. You decide to explain how to save and use favorites by saving the International Travel page on the U.S. Department of State's Web site as a favorite.

STEPS

1. **Click in the Address bar, type travel.state.gov, click the Go button ➡, then click the International Travel link**

   The International Travel page on the U.S. State Department's Web site opens.

2. **Click the Add to Favorites Bar button ⭐ in the row below the Address bar**

   The title of the current Web page is added as the first link in the Favorites Bar. See Figure B-4. The Favorites Bar is a good place to store links to sites you visit often, but it can fill up. You can also add favorites to the Favorites list.

3. **Right-click the Visas link on the Web page, click Open in New Tab on the shortcut menu, click the Visa Home tab, click the Favorites button on the Favorites Bar, then click Add to Favorites in the pane that opens**

   The Add a Favorite dialog box opens. The Name text box shows the text that will be used to identify this Web page in the list of favorites; by default, it is the Web page title. The Create in list box shows the folder in which the favorite will be stored; the default is the main Favorites folder.

TROUBLE

If you have a lot of favorites listed in the Favorites Center on your computer, you might need to scroll down to the bottom of the list to see the new favorite.

4. **Press [Home], type US State Dept, press [Spacebar], then click Add**

   The dialog box closes and the favorite is saved with the name "US State Dept Visa Home."

5. **Click the Home button 🏠 on the Command bar, click the Favorites button, then click the Pin the Favorites Center button ◨ in the pane that opens**

   The start page for your browser appears in the browser window, and the pane listing favorites, called the **Favorites Center**, opens. See Figure B-5. When you add a favorite to the Favorites folder, it appears in this list. The favorite you added is at the bottom of the list of favorites. After you pin the Favorites Center, the browser window resizes to fit next to the Favorites Center, and ◨ changes to the Close the Favorites Center button ✕.

6. **Position the pointer over US State Dept Visa Home in the Favorites Center**

   The pointer changes to 🖑 to indicate that the favorite is a link; the complete URL of the favorite appears in a ScreenTip; and a blue arrow ➡ appears to the right of the favorite name.

QUICK TIP

To open a favorite in a new tab instead of the current tab, click the blue arrow next to the favorite name, or press [Ctrl] while clicking the link.

7. **Click the US State Dept Visa Home link in the Favorites Center**

   The State Department's Visa Home page appears in the current tab.

8. **Right-click the Children & Family link in the current Web page, then click Open in New Tab on the shortcut menu**

   Three pages—the International Travel, Visa Home, and Children and Family Home pages—are open in three tabs in the browser window.

QUICK TIP

To open all the favorites stored in a folder in new tabs, right-click the folder in the Favorites Center, then click Open in Tab Group, or click the blue arrow to the right of the folder in the Favorites Center.

9. **In the Favorites Center, click the Add to Favorites list arrow, click Add Current Tabs to Favorites to open the Add Tabs to Favorites dialog box, type US State Dept General Info in the Folder Name text box, then click Add**

   The dialog box closes and the three pages are added as favorites in a folder named "US State Dept General Info."

10. **Click the US State Dept General Info folder in the Favorites Center**

    The three pages you saved as favorites appear in the Favorites Center below the folder name.

FIGURE B-4: Favorite added to the Favorites Bar

Favorites Bar

New favorite

FIGURE B-5: New favorite listed in the Favorites Center

Favorites button

New favorite

Favorites Center

Pin the Favorites Center button changes to the Close button when the Favorites Center is pinned in place

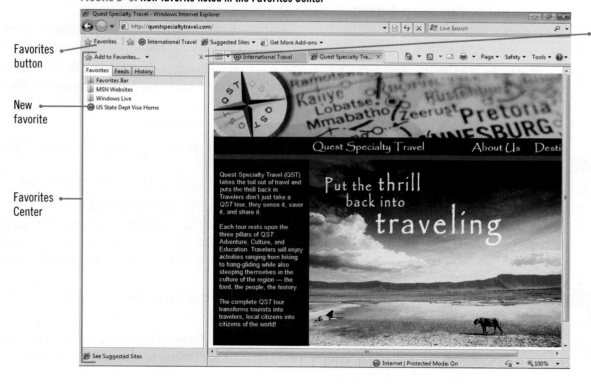

Managing Favorites

You can quickly collect hundreds of favorites as you surf the Web. It's a good idea to organize your favorites into folders so that you can easily find the favorite you are looking for. In the Favorites Center, you can delete and rename favorites, and you can create new folders and move favorites into them. You can also change the order of the favorites in the list. ▟▜▟▛▛ You want to teach the Boston employees how to organize favorites into folders so that they can easily find specific Web pages in their lists of favorites. First, you want to create a folder in which you store Web pages with information about visas.

STEPS

1. **Right-click the US State Dept General Info folder in the Favorites Center, then click Create New Folder on the shortcut menu**

   A new folder appears at the bottom of the list with the temporary folder name "New Folder." See Figure B-6. The folder name is selected, ready for you to type a new name. If you wanted to create a new folder that is not inside another folder, you would right-click a closed folder.

2. **Type Visas, then press [Enter]**

   The folder is renamed. Now you want to move the Visa Home favorite in the US State Dept General Info folder into the new Visas folder.

QUICK TIP

To sort the list in the Favorites Center in alphabetical order, right-click any link or folder, then click Sort by Name on the shortcut menu.

3. **Point to the Visa Home link in the Favorites Center, press and hold the mouse button, then drag the Visa Home link on top of the Visas folder**

   A faint icon depicting the favorite follows the pointer as you drag. See Figure B-7.

4. **Release the mouse button**

   When you release the mouse button, the Visa Home link disappears from the US State Dept General Info folder.

5. **Click the Visas folder in the Favorites Center**

   The Visa Home link appears listed under the Visas folder. Now you want to delete the original favorite you created to the US State Department's Visa Home page because it is a duplicate of the favorite you just moved.

6. **Right-click the US State Dept Visa Home link in the Favorites Center, click Delete, then click Yes in the dialog box that opens asking if you are sure you want to move the file to the Recycle Bin**

   The favorite is deleted. You want to rename the International Travel favorite.

7. **Right-click the International Travel link, click Rename, press [→], press [Spacebar], type Information, then press [Enter]**

   You want to move the folders you created so they appear at the top of the list in the Favorites Center.

TROUBLE

If you can't see the top of the list, position the pointer near the top of the list while you are still holding down the mouse button; the list will scroll up.

8. **Drag the Visas folder up the list in the Favorites Center to the top of the list**

   A faint shadowy icon representing the Visas folder and a horizontal line follow the pointer up the list. The horizontal line indicates where the folder will be positioned in the list when you release the mouse button. The Visas folder appears as the first favorite in the Favorites Center. You can delete folders as well as favorites in the Favorites Center.

TROUBLE

If the folder disappears when you release the mouse button, you probably dropped it into another folder. Open the folders near the top of the list to find the Visas folder.

9. **Right-click the Visas folder, then click Delete on the shortcut menu**

   A dialog box opens asking if you're sure you want to move this folder to the Recycle Bin.

10. **Click Yes in the dialog box, delete the US State Dept General Info folder, right-click the International Travel button on the Favorites Bar, click Delete on the shortcut menu, click Yes, then click the Close button ☒ at the top of the Favorites Center**

    The folders you created in the Favorites Center are deleted, and the Favorites Center closes.

FIGURE B-6: New folder created with temporary name

Selected new folder name

FIGURE B-7: Moving a favorite from one folder to another in the Favorites Center

Favorite being moved

Sharing and backing up your favorites

You can export all of your favorites or any folder in the Favorites Center to a file that you can use as a backup or that you can give to someone else to import. To export your favorites, click the Add to Favorites list arrow at the top of the Favorites Center, then click Import and Export to start the Import/Export Settings wizard. Click the Export to a file option button, then click Next to display the dialog box for selecting what you want to export. Click the Favorites check box, then click Next. In the list in the next dialog box, click the folder you want to export, or click Favorites at the top of the list to export all of your favorites. Click Next to display the dialog box in which you designate a location for the file containing the exported list. The default is to export the favorites to a file named bookmark.htm stored in the Documents folder. If you want to change this, click Browse, navigate to a new folder, replace the filename, then click Save. Click Export, then click Finish. To import this file, click the Import from a file option button in the first dialog box of the Import/Export Settings wizard, click the Favorites check box in the next dialog box, and then select the filename of the list you exported.

Exploring Add-ons

Add-ons, sometimes called **plug-ins** or **extensions**, are programs that add features to Internet Explorer 8. For example, some Web sites provide files for you to read in a format called PDF, and to read PDF files, you need to get the Adobe Acrobat Reader add-on. Some Web sites require add-ons before you can view and browse them. For example, Adobe Flash and Microsoft Silverlight are add-ons that play multimedia files. If you visit a site that requires Flash or Silverlight and that add-on is not installed on your machine, a dialog box opens asking for permission to install it. If you frequently fill out forms when you surf the Web, you could download an add-on to automate this for you. ▰▰▰ Now that the Boston staff is more comfortable with Internet Explorer 8, you teach them how to search for add-ons that will help their productivity.

STEPS

1. **Click Tools on the Command bar, then click Manage Add-ons**

   The Manage Add-ons dialog box opens. See Figure B-8. Toolbars and Extensions is selected in the Add-on Types list on the left, and the list on the right displays add-ons currently loaded in Internet Explorer, as indicated by the Show list box. If you wanted to disable a specific add-on, you could click it in the list, then click Disable at the bottom of the dialog box.

QUICK TIP

You can also click the Get More Add-ons button on the Favorites bar, then click the link in the window that appears to open the Add-ons Gallery.

2. **Click Shockwave Flash Object under Adobe Systems Incorporated in the list on the right.**

   The bottom of the dialog box changes to describe the selected add-on and display the Disable button. See Figure B-9.

3. **Click the Find more toolbars and extensions link**

   A new browser window opens displaying the Add-ons Gallery page on the Windows Internet Explorer 8 Web site. You can browse through the various categories looking for add-ons, or you can type keywords in the Search the Gallery text box to search for specific add-ons.

QUICK TIP

Many Web sites that offer videos or music do not require any add-ons to run because the Web site contains a built in video or audio player.

4. **Maximize the window, if necessary, click in the Search the Gallery text box, type Silverlight, then press [Enter]**

   A list of add-ons that match the search criteria appears in the browser window.

5. **Scroll down, if necessary, then click the Microsoft Silverlight link**

   A Web page describing the Microsoft Silverlight add-on appears in the browser window, along with a command button to add it to Internet Explorer. See Figure B-10.

6. **Click the Close button ▣ in the upper-right corner of the browser window**

   The window closes and the Manage Add-ons dialog box and the original browser window are visible again.

7. **Click Close in the Manage Add-ons dialog box**

   The Manage Add-ons dialog box closes.

FIGURE B-8: Manage Add-ons dialog box

Toolbars and Extensions selected

List of installed add-ons (yours might differ)

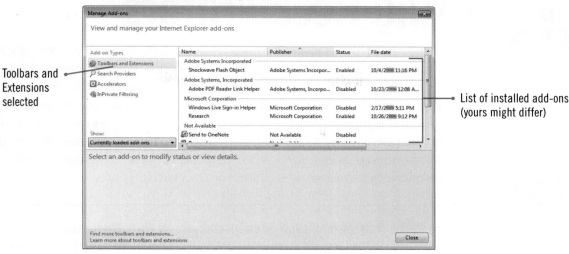

FIGURE B-9: Shockwave add-on selected in the Manage Add-ons dialog box

Selected Shockwave add-on

Information about selected add-on

Click to open Web page listing additional add-ons

Click to disable selected add-on

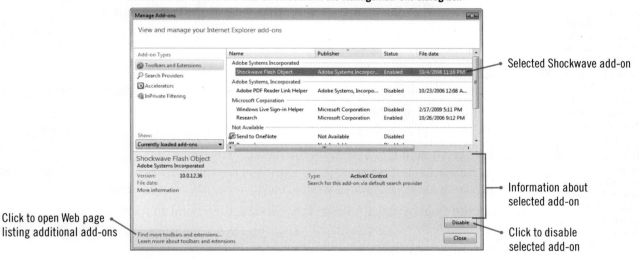

FIGURE B-10: Add-ons Gallery Web page

Address bar identifies the Web site as ieaddons.com

Search the Gallery text box

Add-ons categories

Internet

Using Accelerators

An **Accelerator** is a type of add-on program that is actually a shortcut to another Web site. The Accelerators installed with Internet Explorer 8 by default are listed in Table B-1. To use an Accelerator, you select text or objects on the Web page to display the Accelerator icon. You click the Accelerator icon to see a list of installed Accelerators, and then click the Accelerator you want to use. When you point to some Accelerators on the menu, a small window opens on top of the browser window displaying the result. Other Accelerators require that you click them to open a new tab displaying the Accelerator's Web site. ▟▟▟ Quest employees frequently refer to maps as they examine Web sites related to travel. You explain to them how Accelerators can make looking up information, such as maps, on other Web sites easier.

STEPS

1. **Click in the Address bar, type questspecialtytravel.com, then press [Enter]**
   The home page on the Quest Specialty Travel Web site appears in the current tab.

2. **Click the Destinations link**

3. **Position the pointer to the left of the word Africa, press and hold the left mouse button, drag across the word to highlight it, then release the mouse button**
   The word *Africa* is selected and the Accelerator icon ▱ appears faintly below and to the right of the selected text.

▶ 4. **Click ▱**
   A menu opens listing the installed Accelerators that can be used with the selected text. See Figure B-11.

5. **Point to Map with Live Search on the menu**
   A map appears in a small window on top of the browser window showing Africa. See Figure B-12.

▶ 6. **Click Search with Live Search on the menu**
   The Live Search search provider Web page opens in a new tab displaying "Africa" in the search text box and results for that search listed in the window. You can install additional Accelerators.

7. **Click the Quest Specialty Travel tab, click ▱, then point to All Accelerators**
   A submenu opens listing the installed Accelerators and options for locating and managing Accelerators. If additional Accelerators are installed, they appear on this menu.

8. **Click Find More Accelerators on the submenu**
   The Accelerators page in the Add-ons Gallery on the Windows Internet Explorer 8 Web site opens in the current tab. You can scroll through the list, click one of the category links on the left to filter the list, or use the Search the Gallery text box to search for specific Accelerators.

9. **Click the Back button ◄ to the left of the Address bar**
   The Destinations page on the Quest Specialty Travel Web site appears in the browser window again.

FIGURE B-11: Accelerators menu listing installed Accelerators

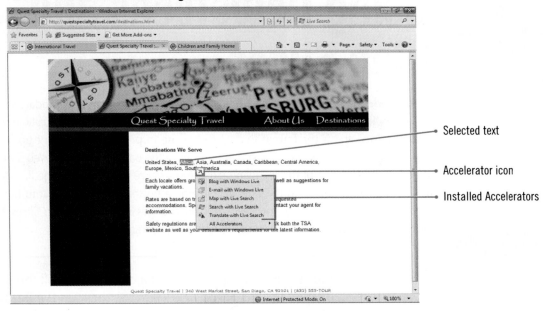

Selected text

Accelerator icon

Installed Accelerators

FIGURE B-12: Map displayed using Map with Live Search Accelerator

Map in window created by Map with Live Search Accelerator

Selected Accelerator

TABLE B-1: Accelerators installed by default

name	site description
Blog with Windows Live	Opens a new blog post in Windows Live
E-mail with Windows Live	Open a new e-mail message in the Windows Live Hotmail program
Map with Live Search	Displays a map of the selected location in Live Search Maps
Search with Live Search	Executes a search in Live Search for the selected text and displays the search results
Translate with Live Search	Displays a translation of the selected text in English if the text is another language and in another language if the text is in English; click the Change Language link to change the language to translate into

Using Newsfeeds and Web Slices

Newsfeeds (or **feeds**) and **Web Slices** are content that is frequently updated and sent to your browser on a regular basis. Both technologies use a form of **RSS**, which usually stands for **Really Simple Syndication**, and is the format that Web sites use to provide the content update. RSS feeds update the whole page; Web Slices update only the portions of the page tagged as a Web Slice. When a Web site offers a feed, it displays one of the following icons somewhere on the Web page: 🔊, RSS, or XML, and usually the Feeds button to the right of the Home button on the Command bar changes to orange. If a Web site offers a Web Slice, the Feeds button changes to the Add Web Slices button 🔲. ☰☰☰ You decide to demonstrate how to subscribe to a newsfeed and a Web Slice.

STEPS

1. **Close all the tabs except one, go to www.sba.gov/advo, scroll through the page and look for XML next to "RSS Feeds," click XML, then, on the Really Simple Syndication page that loads in the browser window, click XML next to "Advocacy What's New"**
   A page describing the feed content available appears in the browser window.

2. **Click the Feeds button 🔊 on the Command bar**
   A page with links to the current stories on the Web site for the Office of Advocacy of the Small Business Administration (SBA) opens in the browser window. See Figure B-13. Text in a yellow box at the top describes newsfeeds. To get the feed from this page, you need to subscribe to it.

3. **Click the Subscribe to this feed link in the yellow box, then click Subscribe in the Subscribe to this Feed dialog box that opens**
   The Web page is updated and the text in the yellow box informs you that you have successfully subscribed.

QUICK TIP

Click a feed in the Favorites Center to open the latest feed.

4. **Click the Favorites button on the Favorites Bar, then click the Feeds tab in the Favorites Center**
   The Feeds section of the Favorites Center opens. The feed you subscribed to is listed.

5. **Right-click Office of Advocacy What's New feed in the Favorites Center, click Delete on the shortcut menu, then click Yes to confirm you want to delete the feed**
   Next you'll subscribe to a Web Slice.

6. **Click in the Address bar, type live.com, press [Enter], then click the News link above the search text box on the Live Search Web page**
   The News page on the Live Search Web site appears, listing headlines. The Feeds button on the Command bar changed to the Web Slices button because this page has Web Slices available.

QUICK TIP

You can also click the Add Web Slices button on the Command bar.

7. **Move the pointer around the Web page until content is highlighted with a green box and the Add Web Slices button 🔲 appears**
   See Figure B-14. This content is tagged as a Web Slice.

8. **Click 🔲, then click Add to Favorites Bar in the Add a Web Slice dialog box that opens**
   The dialog box closes and the Web Slice is added in the first position on the Favorites Bar as a button. It flashes orange briefly to indicate that new content has been found.

QUICK TIP

To subscribe to a newsfeed instead of a Web Slice on a page that offers Web Slices, click the Add Web Slices button list arrow on the Command bar, then click one of the feed options.

9. **Click the Top Stories – Live Search button on the Favorites Bar**
   A small window opens below the button displaying the latest content sliced from the Web page. Click the blue arrow ➔ at the bottom of this window to open the Web page that contains the Web Slice.

10. **Right-click the Top Stories - Live Search button on the Favorites Bar, click Delete on the shortcut menu, then click Yes to confirm moving the Web Slice to the Recycle Bin**

FIGURE B-13: Subscription page for a newsfeed

Click this link to subscribe to this feed

Current stories in feed (the list on your screen will be different)

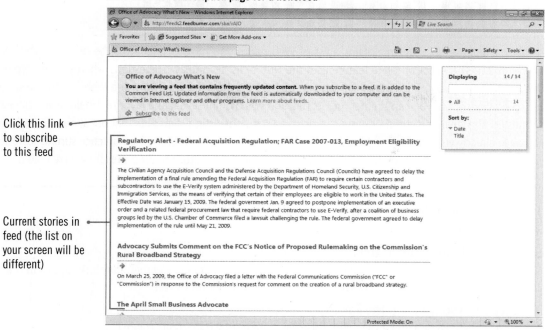

FIGURE B-14: Web Slice displayed from the News page on Live Search

Add Web Slices button on the Command bar

Add Web Slices button in window after pointer is positioned on the content

Content on your screen will differ

Changing feed properties

You can change the properties of a newsfeed that you are subscribed to using the Feed Properties dialog box. You open the dialog box by right-clicking the feed whose properties you want to change on the Feeds tab of the Favorites Center, then clicking Properties on the shortcut menu. Using the settings in this dialog box, you can change the frequency with which the feed is updated from the Web site and the number of feed items to keep in the list. The default is to update once a day and to keep the most recent 200 feed items. You can also determine when a feed was last updated by pointing to the feed name on the Feeds tab in the Favorites Center. A ScreenTip appears telling you the last time the feed was updated.

Using the History List

Recall that Internet Explorer maintains a list of Web pages you have opened and the order in which you viewed them. The AutoComplete feature uses the History list to display suggestions when you are typing a URL in the Address bar. The History list can also be helpful when you want to visit a Web site that you have visited previously, but you can't remember its URL and you did not save it as a favorite. Finally, if you have the Suggested Sites feature turned on, you can open a Web page listing Web sites that are similar to Web sites you have already visited. ▰▰▰▰ Now that the staff in the Boston office have had practice surfing to various Web sites, you decide to show them how to use the History list to return to Web sites they have visited.

STEPS

1. **Click the Favorites button in the bar below the Address bar**
   The Favorites Center opens.

2. **Click the History tab in the Favorites Center**
   View By Date appears in the list box at the top of the Favorites Center, and the Today link appears in the list. You might also see links for Yesterday, Last Week, 2 Weeks Ago, and so on.

3. **Click the Today link in the Favorites Center**
   A list of the Web sites you visited today opens represented by folders. See Figure B-15.

4. **Scroll down the list if necessary, then click the live (www.live.com) folder**
   A link to the Live Search Web page appears below the folder you clicked. This is the Web page on the live.com site that you visited earlier in this unit.

5. **Click the View By Date list arrow at the top of the Favorites Center**
   The menu that opens provides commands for changing the History list so that it is sorted alphabetically by Web site, in the order most visited to least visited, or sorted in the order you visited today.

6. **Click View By Order Visited Today**
   The list changes to show you only the Web pages that you visited today, in order from most recently visited to first visited.

7. **Click the View By Order Visited Today list arrow, click Search History, click in the Search for text box that appears, type quest specialty, then click Search Now**
   At least two of the pages on the Quest Specialty Travel Web site are listed: the Home page and the Destinations page.

8. **At the bottom of the Favorites Center, click the See Suggested Sites link**
   The Favorites Center closes and the Suggested Sites page on Microsoft's Web site opens in the browser window listing additional sites you might like based on the current Web page and your browsing history. See Figure B-16.

9. **Click the Back button ⬅ to the left of the Address bar, then click the Suggested Sites button on the Favorites Bar**
   A small window opens displaying a short list of sites that are similar to the Web page currently displayed in the browser window.

FIGURE B-15: List of Web sites visited today in the Favorites Center

History tab

History list
(your list
might differ)

Live.com Web site
in History list

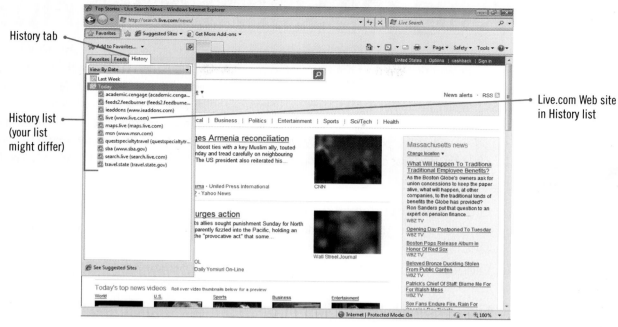

FIGURE B-16: Suggested Sites Web page

Most recently
viewed Web page

Your suggested
sites might differ

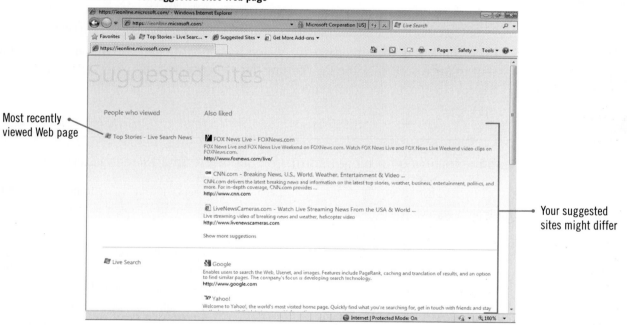

Deleting your browsing history

There are times when you may want to remove all traces of your browsing history, for example, if you are using a public computer in an Internet café or at a library. To do this, click the Safety button on the Command bar, and then click Delete Browsing History to open the Delete Browsing History dialog box. (You can also open this dialog box by clicking the Tools button on the Command bar, clicking Internet Options, and then clicking Delete in the Browsing history section on the General tab in the Internet Options dialog box.) At the top, the default is for the Preserve Favorites website data check box

to be selected. This means that cookies, which you will learn about in the next lesson, and temporary Internet files associated with your Favorites will not be deleted. If you want to delete that information, you must click this check box to deselect it. Below this option, you can select the individual elements you want to delete. The default choices are to delete temporary Internet files, cookies, and history, and to not delete form data, saved passwords, and InPrivate filtering data. After you make your selections, click Delete.

Using the SmartScreen Filter

A **phishing site**, sometimes called a **spoofed site**, is a Web site set up to look like another Web site, such as a bank's Web site, but does not actually belong to the organization portrayed in the site. Phishing sites are set up to try to convince customers they are visiting the real site so they enter personal information, such as credit card numbers, Social Security numbers, and passwords. The thief collecting the information can then use it to steal the customer's money or identity. The **SmartScreen Filter** checks to see if the Web site you are visiting is a phishing site. 🔲 You want everyone in the Boston office to be aware of some of the security risks that come with using the Internet, so you teach them about the SmartScreen Filter.

STEPS

1. **Click the Safety button on the Command bar, then point to SmartScreen Filter**
   A submenu opens. The second command in the menu is either Turn Off SmartScreen Filter or Turn On SmartScreen Filter.

2. **Click Turn Off SmartScreen Filter or Turn On SmartScreen Filter**
   The Microsoft SmartScreen Filter dialog box opens. See Figure B-17.

3. **Click the Close button 🔳 in the upper-right corner of the dialog box**
   The dialog box closes and the status of the SmartScreen Filter is unchanged.

4. **Click the empty box immediately to the left of the Security Settings button 🌐 in the status bar**
   A shortcut menu opens with the same commands you saw on the SmartScreen Filter submenu in Step 1.

5. **Click Check This Website, then, if a dialog box opens telling you that information will be sent to Microsoft, click the Don't show this again check box to deselect it, then click OK**
   A dialog box opens telling you that this site has not been reported as a threat.

6. **Click OK**

DETAILS

Read the following for more information about the SmartScreen Filter:

- When the SmartScreen Filter is turned on, it analyzes Web pages and URLs to see if they have characteristics of phishing sites. It also sends the URLs of Web pages you visit to Microsoft to be compared against the latest list of known phishing sites.

- If the SmartScreen Filter determines that the Web page you are trying to visit matches one of the sites listed as a phishing site or has the characteristics of a phishing site, the Address bar is colored red, a notification in the Address bar flags the site as an unsafe Web site, the background in the browser window is colored red, and a message informing you that this Web site has been reported as unsafe appears. See Figure B-18.

- If a Web site is not on the list of known phishing sites, Internet Explorer checks to see if the Web page has the characteristics of a phishing site. If it does, a notification appears in a window titled "Are you trying to visit this website?" and the domain name of the Web site is highlighted in a large box below the title. A yellow shield with an exclamation point on it also appears in the Address bar that you can click to display the notification window. Cick Yes to report to Microsoft that the address is correct, or No to report the Web site as unsafe.

- If you receive an e-mail purporting to be a company with which you do business asking you to click a link to verify personal identification information, don't click the link. Instead, open a new browser window, type the URL of the company directly into the Address bar, and check your account information in the usual way. If you receive an e-mail from a company with whom you do not do business telling you that your account has been compromised or asking you to check your account status, again, do not click the link in the e-mail. If you want to follow up with the company, open a new browser window and contact them directly.

FIGURE B-17: Microsoft SmartScreen Filter dialog box

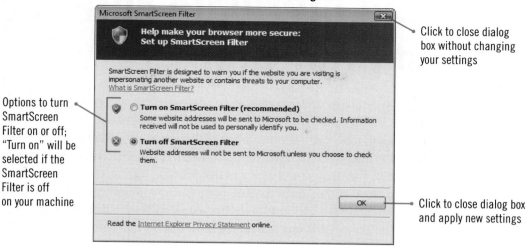

Click to close dialog box without changing your settings

Options to turn SmartScreen Filter on or off; "Turn on" will be selected if the SmartScreen Filter is off on your machine

Click to close dialog box and apply new settings

FIGURE B-18: Internet Explorer 8 window indicating a known phishing site

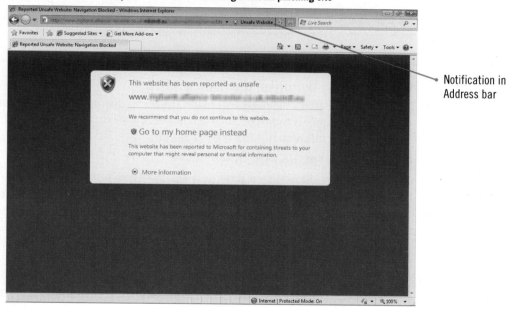

Notification in Address bar

Controlling cookies

Cookies are small text files that a Web site stores on your computer. Cookies contain information that identifies you to the Web server and tells the Web server when you visited. If you clicked a link on another Web site to get to the site, cookies can help tell the server which site you came from; cookies can also identify the links you click as you navigate the Web site and which link you click to navigate away from the site. Some cookies store things such as your username for a Web site or items you place in a shopping cart on a Web site. Other cookies are placed to track the Web sites you visit to generate marketing data. Cookies can be accessed and read only by the Web site that placed them on your computer. Some Web sites, however, have agreements with marketing companies that allow the marketing company to place images on a Web site; these images are linked to the marketing company's site. This means the marketing company can also place a cookie on your computer. Any time you visit any site on which the marketing company has an image, the marketing company's cookie sends data back to the marketing company. To control cookies, click the Tools button on the Command bar, click Internet Options, and then click the Privacy tab. Drag the slider to change the setting, and click Sites to open the Per Site Privacy Actions dialog box to add specific sites from which you will always allow or always block cookies. If you visit a site and cookies are blocked, ⬚ appears in the status bar.

Using InPrivate Filtering and Browsing

Many Web pages contain content provided by companies other than the company or person who owns the Web page. This is commonly referred to as **third-party content**. This content can include advertisements and analysis tools that determine which Web site you are visiting and track your clicks on the page. **InPrivate Filtering**, which is turned off by default, analyzes the content on Web pages you visit, and if the same content is used on several Web sites that you visit, you can choose to block that content. You can also choose to block all third-party content, but this might prevent you from accessing content that you want to view on some Web sites. **InPrivate Browsing** is a feature that allows you to open a new browser window and surf the Web without leaving the usual trail on your computer; that is, the sites you visit will not be recorded in the History list and will not appear on the Address bar AutoComplete list or the Search box suggestions list, and files stored in the Temporary Internet Files folder and cookies recorded are automatically deleted when you close the InPrivate Browsing window. Note that many add-ons and third-party toolbars are turned off when using InPrivate Browsing. Several people in the Boston office have asked if there's any way they can prevent third-party sites from collecting information about them as they visit Web sites. You explain InPrivate Filtering and InPrivate Browsing.

STEPS

1. **Click the** Safety button **on the Command bar**

   The InPrivate Filtering command appears on the menu that opens. If a check mark appears next to the command, the feature is turned on. If there is no check mark next to the command, the feature is turned off. The default is for InPrivate Filtering to be turned off.

TROUBLE

If this is the first time you have clicked this command and if InPrivate Filtering is turned off, the InPrivate Filtering dialog box opens. Click Block for me, repeat Steps 1 and 2, then click the Off option button.

2. **Click** InPrivate Filtering Settings

   The InPrivate Filtering settings dialog box opens. See Figure B-19. The option button selected above the list box depends on your InPrivate settings. The default is for InPrivate Filtering to be turned off. If any content is being filtered, it appears in the list. Below the list box is a box that contains the number of sites you visit that can share content before the content from that provider is blocked.

3. **Click** OK

   The dialog box closes.

QUICK TIP

You can also open a new tab, then click the Open an InPrivate Browsing window link.

4. **Click the** Safety button **on the Command bar, then click** InPrivate Browsing

   A new browser window opens with the InPrivate indicator in the Address bar. See Figure B-20. Any Web sites you visit using this browser window will not be tracked in your History list and will not be able to store cookies on your computer. (Note that Web sites can still place cookies on your computer so that you can use Web sites that require cookies; these cookies are deleted after you leave the site.)

5. **Click in the** Address bar, **type** boston.com, **then press** [Enter]

   The home page of the Boston.com Web site loads in the browser window.

TROUBLE

If you have visited Boston.com previously, the list below the Address bar will display suggestions that include this Web site.

6. **Click the** Home button 🏠 **on the Command bar, click in the** Address bar, **then type** bos

   Notice that the list that appears below the Address bar does not suggest Boston.com as you type.

7. **Click the** Favorites button **on the Favorites Bar, click the** History tab, **click the** View By Order Visited Today **list arrow, then click** View By Site

   The History list is resorted in alphabetical order by Web sites that you visited today. Notice that Boston.com does not appear in this list.

8. **Click the** Close button ❌ **in the InPrivate Browsing window title bar**

   The InPrivate Browsing window closes and the standard browser window is in view again.

FIGURE B-19: InPrivate Filtering settings dialog box

Click option to select filtering setting

Filtered content would appear here

Number of sites you visit that can share content before being added to the blocked list

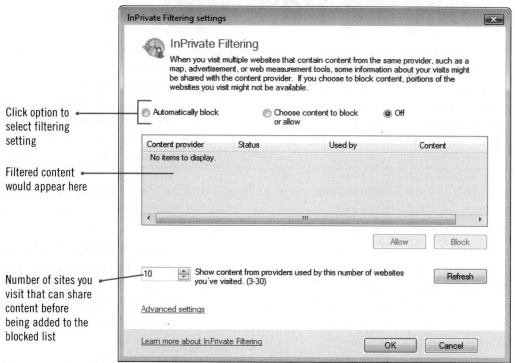

FIGURE B-20: New InPrivate Browsing window

Identifies window as InPrivate browsing session

Examining the privacy policy of a Web page

To exert more control over which cookies you allow a Web site to place on your computer, click the Safety button on the Command bar, and then click Webpage Privacy Policy to open the Privacy Report dialog box. This dialog box lists all the Web sites that have content on the current Web page. It also indicates whether you have specifically accepted or blocked cookies from those Web sites. You can view a summary of a Web site's privacy policy by clicking the site in the list, and then clicking Summary to open the Privacy Policy dialog box. If the site has a privacy policy, it appears in the dialog box; otherwise, a message appears telling you that Internet Explorer could not find a privacy policy for that site. You can then click option buttons to always allow this site to use cookies, never allow this site to use cookies, or compare the privacy policy to your settings, which is the default option.

Managing Pop-ups

Some Web sites allow **pop-ups**, content that appears in a new browser window. Sometimes pop-ups contain advertisements, and sometimes pop-ups contain legitimate content from the Web site you are viewing. Internet Explorer blocks most pop-ups. You can use the **Pop-up Blocker** to control this behavior and allow pop-ups from specific Web sites. ▄▄▄▄ Keisha Lane, the vice president of operations, wants the library of reference books in the Boston office to be expanded. You decide to teach the staff how to manage pop-ups as you look for books to purchase.

STEPS

TROUBLE

If nothing happens when you click the Pop-up Blocker Settings command, click Turn On Pop-up Blocker, then repeat Step 1. Turn the Pop-up Blocker off after you complete Step 9.

1. **Click Tools on the Command bar, point to Pop-up Blocker, then click Pop-up Blocker Settings**

   The Pop-up Blocker Settings dialog box opens, similar to Figure B-21.

2. **Make sure the Show Information Bar when a pop-up is blocked check box is selected, click the Blocking level list arrow, click High: Block all pop-ups (Ctrl+Alt to override), if necessary, then click Close**

   The default setting is Medium, which blocks pop-ups that open without your permission, but allows pop-ups to open as a result of you clicking a link. Setting the filter level to High means that all pop-ups will be blocked.

TROUBLE

If the Information Bar dialog box opens in the middle of the window, click Close in the dialog box.

3. **Go to www.hospitality-tourism.delmar.cengage.com in the current tab, click the Travel & Tourism link in the Web page that opens, then click the Conducting Tours link**

   The Travel & Tourism page on the Delmar Cengage Learning Web site opens, and the yellow Information bar appears at the top of the browser window telling you that the pop-up was blocked. An icon 🖼 in the status bar also indicates that a pop-up was blocked. See Figure B-22. If you don't want to allow the pop-up to open, you can ignore the Information bar after you close the dialog box, or you can close it by clicking the Close button ✖ at the right end of the Information bar.

QUICK TIP

You can also press [Ctrl][Alt] while you click a link to override the Pop-up Blocker.

4. **Click the Information bar**

   A menu opens. The Information bar appears under several different circumstances, and the menu changes to offer choices relevant to the circumstances. In this case, you can choose to allow pop-ups from this Web site or to allow pop-ups temporarily.

5. **Click Always Allow Pop-ups from This Site on the menu, then click Yes in the confirmation dialog box that appears**

   The contents of the window **refresh**, or reload in the browser window.

6. **Click the Conducting Tours link again**

   A new browser window opens displaying information about a book, *Conducting Tours, A Practical Guide*. The icon on the status bar in the original window changes to 🖼 to indicate that a pop-up was allowed.

QUICK TIP

You can also click 🖼 in the status bar, then click Pop-up Blocker Settings.

7. **Click the Tools button on the Command bar in the new browser window, point to Pop-up Blocker, then click Pop-up Blocker Settings**

   The Pop-up Blocker Settings dialog box opens.

8. **Click *.delmar.cengage.com in the Allowed sites list, then click Remove**

   The Web site is removed from the list of sites allowed to display pop-ups no matter what the Filter level is.

9. **If necessary, click the Filter level list arrow, click the original setting for your browser, then click Close**

   The dialog box closes, and the Pop-up Blocker settings on your computer are returned to their original status.

FIGURE B-21: Pop-up Blocker Settings dialog box

Type a URL here to allow it to display pop-ups

List of allowed sites; your list might contain URLs

Click to add URL to Allowed sites list

Click to change the filter level

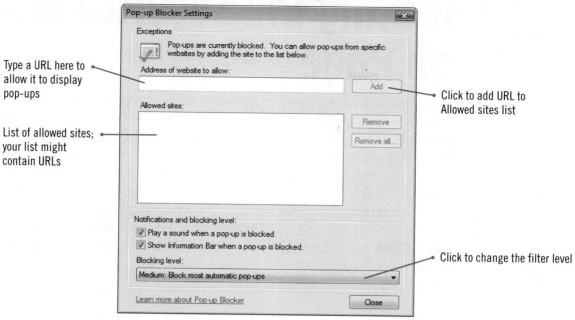

FIGURE B-22: Web page when a pop-up is blocked

Information bar when a pop-up is blocked

Conducting Tours link

Indicates that a pop-up is blocked

Close button

Reopening the last browser session

If you want to reopen your last browser session, you can click the Tools button on the Command bar, then click Reopen Last Browsing Session. All the tabs that were open when you exited Internet Explorer the last time you used it reopen in new tabs.

Checking the Security of a Web Page

When you can purchase goods or services from a Web site, you generally need to provide sensitive financial information, such as a credit card number, expiration date, and billing address. Almost all sites that request such financial information on the Web do it securely, but you should always verify this. The URL of a secure Web page usually begins with *https* instead of *http*. The *s* stands for "secure." And in Internet Explorer, when you open a secure Web page, a padlock icon 🔒 appears in the Address bar. As part of the HTTPS protocol, Web sites must have digital certificates for a browser to examine when it loads the secure Web page. Digital **certificates** identify the URL of the Web page, the name of the certification company that verified the Web site, and the expiration date for the certificate. Certificates are issued by **certificate authorities**. ▬▬▬ You will show how to check the security of a Web page by placing a book in the shopping cart.

STEPS

1. **In the window that contains the information about the book, *Conducting Tours: A Practical Guide*, scroll down, if necessary, then click Add to Cart to add the book to the shopping cart**

   The Web page changes to display the shopping cart for this Web site. It lists the book you just added.

2. **Click Continue Checkout**

   The Billing/Shipping page opens. This is the page on which you would enter your personal information if you were to buy this book. You can tell that it is a secure page because the padlock icon 🔒 appears in the Address bar, and the protocol at the beginning of the URL is "https."

3. **Maximize the window, if necessary, then click 🔒 in the Address bar**

   A Website Identification report is displayed in a box just under the Address bar. It identifies the Web site and informs you that the connection is **encrypted**, which means data sent over the connection is coded so that only the Web site with the code can read it. See Figure B-23.

4. **Click View certificates in the Website Identification box**

   The Website Identification report closes and the Certificate dialog box opens with the General tab on top. See Figure B-24. You can see the dates between which the current certificate is valid.

5. **Click OK to close the Certificate dialog box**

   If there were a problem with the certificate—for example, if it was expired or if it were revoked—the Address bar would be colored red, and a notification in the Address bar would tell you that there was a certificate error. You can click that notification to display the security report detailing the error.

6. **Click the Close button ❌ in the upper-right corner of the browser window to cancel the transaction and close the browser window**

7. **Click the Close button ❌ on the title bar to exit Internet Explorer**

FIGURE B-23: Website Identification report on a secure Web page

Indicates the Web page is secure

Website Identification report

Click to view digital certificate for this site

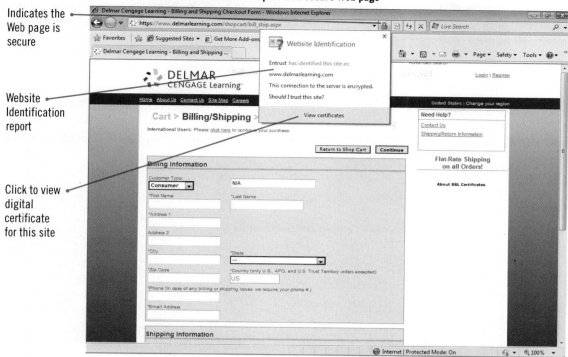

FIGURE B-24: Certificate dialog box

Certificate owner

Certificate authority

Dates between which the certificate is valid (might be different on your screen)

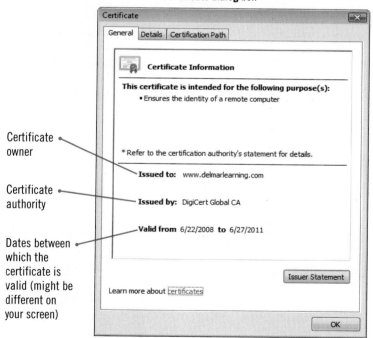

Understanding Extended Validation certificates

Some Web site owners have paid for an Extended Validation SSL certificate. This means that the site has undergone extensive testing by the certificate authority to verify that it is a legitimate site. If a site has an Extended Validation SSL certificate, the Address bar will be colored green, and the name of the company that owns the certificate and the name of the certificate authority will appear to the right of the padlock icon in the Address bar.

Practice

If you have a SAM user profile, you may have access to hands-on instruction, practice, and assessment of the skills covered in this unit. Log in to your SAM account (http://sam2007.course.com/) to launch any assigned training activities or exams that relate to the skills covered in this unit.

▼ CONCEPTS REVIEW

Label each component of the Internet Explorer program windows shown in Figures B-25 and B-26.

FIGURE B-25

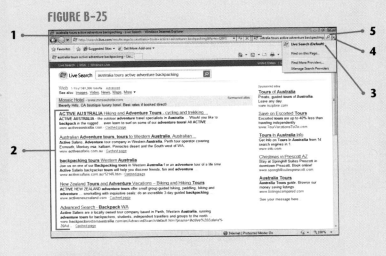

FIGURE B-26

Match each term with the statement that best describes it.

11. **certificate**

12. **InPrivate Browsing**

13. **InPrivate Filtering**

14. **add-ons**

15. **Pop-up Blocker**

16. **newsfeed**

17. **SmartScreen Filter**

a. Checks to see if the Web site you are visiting is a legitimate site

b. Identifies the URL of a Web page, the name of the certification company that verified the Web site, and the expiration date for the certificate

c. A list of links to updated headlines that is sent to your browser on a regular basis

d. Allows you to control the behavior of pop-ups

e. Analyzes the content on Web pages you visit, and allows you to block that content

f. A feature that allows you to open a new browser window and surf the Web without leaving a trail on your computer

g. Programs that add features to Internet Explorer

Select the best answer from the list of choices.

18. To quickly open Web pages you have visited before, you can save them to the:

   a. Favorites Bar   **c.** status bar

   b. Favorites Web site   **d.** Feed bar

19. An add-on program that is a shortcut to another Web site is a(n):

   a. Administrator   **c.** Feed program

   b. Accelerator   **d.** Slice provider

20. A feed is one example of content that you ask to be sent to your browser on a regular basis, and a(n) _____ is another.

   a. Slice of the Web   **c.** Web Slice

   b. Active Favorite   **d.** None of the above

21. When you cause a browser to load the content of a Web page in the window again, it is called:

   a. managing   **c.** refreshing

   b. redoing   **d.** rebrowsing

22. A Web site set up to look like another Web site for the purpose of illegally obtaining personal or financial information is called a:

   a. certificate site   **c.** phishing site

   b. pop-up site   **d.** pretend site

23. Small text files that a Web site stores on your computer are called:

   a. phishes   **c.** cookies

   b. favorites   **d.** certificates

24. Content that appears in a new browser window is called a:

   a. blocked site   **c.** phishing site

   b. pop-up   **d.** secure site

25. The icon that appears in the Address bar when a Web site is secure is a:

   a. padlock   **c.** yellow exclamation point

   b. certificate   **d.** large letter "s"

26. When a Web site is on the list of known phishing sites, the Address bar is colored:

   a. red   **c.** white

   b. yellow   **d.** green

27. The Web page that opens as a result of a search is called a:

   a. search results page   **c.** sponsored results page

   b. search provider page   **d.** Favorite page

28. According to the text, RSS stands for:

   a. Refreshed Simple Stories   **c.** Really Simple Syndication

   b. Real Standard Stories   **d.** Resulting Story Syndication

▼ SKILLS REVIEW

1. **Use the Search box.**
   a. Start Internet Explorer, then use the Search box to search for Web pages that contain the keywords **Canadian rail tours**. Note the number of results found.
   b. Narrow the search by adding **Rockies** to the search expression.
   c. Open the Web page that lists additional search providers you can add to your browser.
   d. Open the Manage Add-ons dialog box to display the list of search providers currently installed on your computer.
   e. Close the Manage Add-ons dialog box, then use the Back button to go back to the search results page.

2. **Create and use favorites.**
   a. Right-click one of the search results, then open it in a new tab.
   b. Save the Canadian Rockies rail tour search results page to the Favorites Bar.
   c. Save the same page, the Canadian Rockies rail tour search results page, as a favorite named **Canada Rail Suggestions** in the Favorites Center.
   d. Save the current tabs in a folder named **Rockies Tours**.
   e. Open the Favorites Center and pin it into place.
   f. Close either of the tabs, then open your browser's start page in the tab that's left open.
   g. Open the Canada Rail Suggestions favorite in the current tab.
   h. Expand the Rockies Tours folder in the Favorites Center.

3. **Manage favorites.**
   a. Create a new folder within the Rockies Tours folder in the Favorites Center named **Tours**.
   b. Drag the two favorites stored in the Rockies Tours folder in the Favorites Center into the Tours folder.
   c. Rename the Tours folder to **Rail Tours**.
   d. Drag the Rail Tours folder up so it is the second folder in the list.
   e. Delete the Rockies Tours folder.
   f. Delete the Rail Tours folder and the Canada Rail Suggestions favorite, then close the Favorites Center.
   g. Delete the Canadian rail tours Rockies button on the Favorites Bar.

4. **Explore add-ons.**
   a. Go to **www.ieaddons.com** in the current tab.
   b. Click several of the category links on the left.
   c. Click in the Search the Gallery text box, type **delicious**, then press [Enter]. Scroll down the list of results, if necessary, until you see Delicious Bookmarks Add-on, then click its link.
   d. Go to **www.flashgallery.co.uk**. If you have the Flash add-on, you will see "YOU HAVE FLASH" in the middle of the screen, above the ENTER SITE graphic, and animated bars moving across it. If you don't have the Flash add-on, you won't see anything above the ENTER SITE graphic.
   e. Go to www.silverlight.net/Showcase. If you have the Silverlight add-on, you will see a palette of thumbnails linking to Web sites that have Silverlight content. If you don't have the Silverlight add-on, a dialog box will appear offering to let you install Silverlight.
   f. If the dialog box is open asking if you want to install Silverlight, click the Close button in the upper-right corner to close it.

5. **Use Accelerators.**

   a. Go to **www.nytimes.com**.

   b. Drag to select the name of a city, state, or country, then use the Map with Live Search Accelerator to display a map of the location.

   c. Select a phrase or sentence, then use the Translate with Live Search Accelerator to translate it into another language (use the default language).

   d. With the same phrase or sentence selected, use the Search with Live Search Accelerator to display search results using the selected text as the search expression.

6. **Use newsfeeds and Web Slices.**

   a. Close all tabs but one, then go to **news.bbc.co.uk**.

   b. Subscribe to the newsfeed on this page. Rename it **BBC World News**.

   c. Go to **www.msn.com**.

   d. Add the Web Slice on this page to the Favorites Bar.

   e. Open the Feeds tab in the Favorites Center, then display the latest headlines using the BBC World News feed.

   f. Display the Web Slice in a window.

   g. Delete the MSN.com Web Slice on the Favorites Bar and delete the BBC World News feed from the Feeds tab in the Favorites Center.

7. **Use the History list.**

   a. Open the History list in the Favorites Center, then pin the Favorites Center in place.

   b. Change the list so that you are viewing the list by date, and then expand the list to display the sites visited today.

   c. Search the History list for sites or Web pages containing **BBC**.

   d. Display the sites in order visited today.

   e. Open the Suggested Sites Web page.

   f. Close the Favorites Center.

8. **Use the SmartScreen Filter.**

   a. Open the Microsoft SmartScreen Filter dialog box.

   b. Click the "What is SmartScreen Filter?" link at the top of the dialog box to open a Help window. Click some of the arrows or plus signs next to topics to read about the SmartScreen Filter. Close the Help window when you are finished.

   c. Close the Microsoft SmartScreen Filter window without changing the setting.

   d. Click the Safety button on the Command bar, point to SmartScreen Filter, then click Check This Website. If a dialog box opens asking you to confirm that you know that information will be sent to Microsoft, click the Don't show this message again check box to deselect it, then click OK. Wait for the process to complete.

   e. In the dialog box that appears telling you that the current Web page is not a reported phishing Web site, click OK.

9. **Use InPrivate Filtering and Browsing.**

   a. Open the InPrivate Filtering settings dialog box.

   b. Click the Advanced settings link in the dialog box.

   c. Close the Manage Add-ons dialog box.

   d. Click the Learn more about InPrivate Filtering link.

   e. Click several of the links in the Help window that opens, read the information, then close the Help window.

   f. Close the InPrivate Filtering settings dialog box without changing the settings.

   g. Open an InPrivate Browsing window.

   h. Close the InPrivate Browsing window.

Internet

10. Manage pop-ups.

   a. Open the Pop-up Blocker Settings dialog box, change the filter level to High, if necessary, and select the check box to show the Information bar, if necessary.

   b. Go to **msnbc.msn.com** in the current tab.

   c. Click the Video link. On the page that opens, click one of the still photographs from a video.

   d. Click the Information bar, and allow pop-ups from this site.

   e. Click the still photo again to verify that the pop-up window opens. Close the new window.

   f. Open the Pop-up Blocker Settings dialog box, then remove the msnbc.msn site from the list of allowed sites.

   g. Change the filter level back to its original level, then close the dialog box.

11. Check the security of a Web page.

   a. Go to **www.bn.com** in the current tab.

   b. Search for an item that interests you, and add it to the shopping cart.

   c. Click the Proceed to Checkout button.

   d. In the page that opens, click the padlock icon in the Address bar.

   e. View the digital certificate for the site.

   f. Close the Certificate dialog box, then close the current tab to cancel the transaction.

   g. Exit Internet Explorer.

▼ INDEPENDENT CHALLENGE 1

You run your town's youth basketball league. You need to find new suppliers for trophies and uniforms.

   a. Start Internet Explorer.

   b. Type a search expression in the Search box to help you locate Web sites that sell trophies and awards.

   c. Open three of the pages you find in new tabs.

   d. On each tab, find and select the address of the Web site owner, then use the Map with Live Search Accelerator to display maps of the locations.

   e. Save the tabs in a folder named **Trophies**.

   f. Search for Web sites that sell uniforms for youth sports leagues.

   g. Open three of the pages you find in new tabs.

   h. Save the tabs in a folder named **Uniforms**.

   i. Create a new folder in the Favorites Center named **League Info**.

   j. Move the Trophies and Uniforms folders into the League Info folder.

   k. Move the League Info folder to the top of the list in the Favorites Center.

   l. Delete the League Info folder from the Favorites Center.

   m. Close all open tabs and exit Internet Explorer.

▼ INDEPENDENT CHALLENGE 2

Phishing is a growing threat to people who use the Internet. Several companies are trying to combat this phenomenon. You decide to do a little more research so that you can be prepared.

a. Start Internet Explorer.

b. Go to **www.phishtank.com**.

c. Click the FAQ link (FAQ stands for Frequently Asked Questions). Click a few of the question links and read more about phishing and what the PhishTank site does.

d. Go to **www.bankersonline.com/phishing/**, then subscribe to the news service feed on this site; name it **Anti-Phishing News**.

Advanced Challenge Exercise

- Change the frequency of the newsfeed updates to once every hour.
- Change the maximum number of updates you want to save to 125.
- Change the settings so that a sound is played when a feed is found on a Web page.

e. Click the Get More Add-ons button on the Favorites Bar, click the Find more in the Internet Explorer Add-ons Gallery link to open the Add-ons Gallery Web page, then search for **Tech Topics**.

f. Add the Tech Topics on SitePoint Web Slice to the Favorites Bar.

g. Display the Web Slice in the small window.

h. Open an InPrivate Browsing window, go to **www.millersmiles.co.uk**, then click a few links on this Web site.

i. Close the InPrivate Browsing window, then open the History list. Confirm that www.millersmiles.co.uk does not appear in the list.

j. Delete the newsfeed from the Feeds tab in the Favorites Center, then delete the Web Slice from the Favorites Bar.

k. Close all open tabs and exit Internet Explorer.

▼ INDEPENDENT CHALLENGE 3

You want to add more functionality to your browser, so you decide to examine the add-ons available.

    a. Start Internet Explorer.

    b. Go to **www.ieaddons.com**.

    c. Click the Most Popular link and examine the first page of results.

    d. Click the links for any that look interesting, and save the pages that describe them as favorites to the Favorites Bar or in the Favorites Center.

Advanced Challenge Exercise

- Choose the add-on that you think would be the most helpful, display it in the browser window, then click Add to Internet Explorer.
- In the dialog box that opens, click Add. (If a dialog box with an Add command button does not open, close the window that opens, and then select a different add-on.)
- Open the Manage Add-ons dialog box, find and select the add-on you just installed in the list, then click Disable or Remove. You might need to click a different selection in the Add-on Types list on the left side of the dialog box. (Note that the program you install might create several add-ons. Disable or remove all of them.) Close the Manage Add-ons dialog box.
- If you were only able to disable the add-on rather than remove it, and if you are working in a lab or you want to uninstall this add-on from your computer, exit Internet Explorer, click the Start button, click Control Panel, click Programs, click Uninstall a program under Programs and Features, then locate and click the add-on in the list, (if you don't see it in the list, click View installed updates in the Tasks list on the left). Click Uninstall or Uninstall/ Change on the toolbar, click Continue in the User Account Control dialog box, and then click Yes in the warning dialog box if it appears.

    e. Return to the Home page on ieaddons.com, then add the Web Slice on that page to the Favorites Bar.

    f. Delete the Web Slice from your Favorites Bar, and then delete any favorites you added on the Favorites Bar or to the Favorites Center.

    g. Close all open tabs and exit Internet Explorer.

▼ REAL LIFE INDEPENDENT CHALLENGE

There are Web sites from which you can purchase custom personalized items, everything from T-shirts to mugs to stamps to candy. Search for several of these sites and save them as favorites in case you decide to throw a party or want to purchase a personalized present for someone.

a. Start Internet Explorer.

b. Conduct a search for **custom T-shirts**, **custom candy**, and so on. Add the phrase **no minimum** as part of the search expression.

c. Save at least four pages as favorites in the Favorites Center.

d. Create a folder in the Favorites Center, name it appropriately, then move the favorites you created into the new folder.

e. Go to one of the sites you saved as a favorite, place an item in the shopping cart, and then navigate to the first secure checkout page on the site.

f. Display the digital certificate for the site.

g. Close the Certificate dialog box.

h. Delete the favorites you added to the Favorites Center.

i. Close all open tabs, and then exit Internet Explorer.

Internet

▼ VISUAL WORKSHOP

Practice the skills you learned in this lesson to create the screen shown in Figure B-27. Start by using the Search box to search for pages listing volunteer opportunities sponsored by the United States government. Save the three Web pages shown in Figure B-27 as favorites in a folder named Volunteering. Move the folder so it appears second in the list as in the figure, and then open the folder. Save the USAJOBS.gov page as a favorite on the Favorites Bar. When you are finished, delete the favorites you added to the Favorites Center and the Favorites Bar.

FIGURE B-27

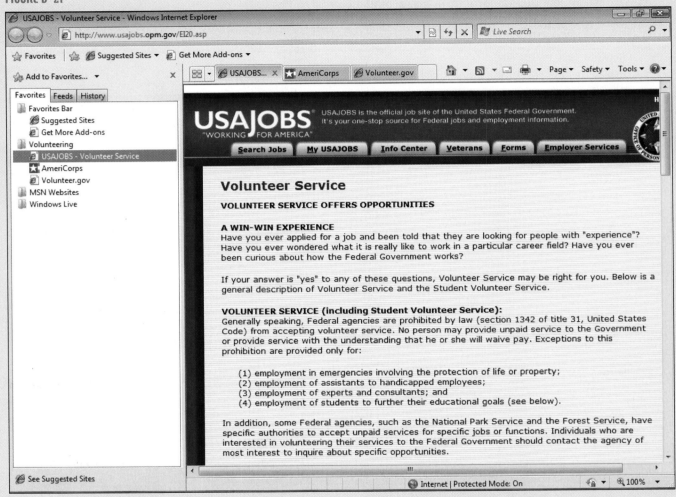

Glossary

Accelerator A type of add-on program that is actually a shortcut to another Web site.

Active tab The tab on top of other tabs in a browser window.

Add-on A program that adds features to Internet Explorer; *also called* extension or plug-in.

Address bar The element in Internet Explorer at the top of the program window that shows the complete URL of the Web page currently open in the browser window and in which you can type a new URL.

AutoComplete A feature in Internet Explorer that opens a list of URLs in the Address bar that match previously typed URLs, or pages in the History list or saved Favorites.

Browse To use a browser to look for and view Web pages; *also called* surf.

Browser *See* Web browser.

Browser window The program window for a browser in which Web pages appear.

Certificate *See* digital certificate.

Certificate authority A business that issues digital certificates.

Command bar A toolbar located on the right side of the Internet Explorer window just below the Search box.

Compatibility view For use with Web pages that have not been updated to the lastest Web standards, a view that displays the Web page as if viewed in an older browser so that it can be viewed as it was designed.

Compatibility View Updates A setting in Internet Explorer 8 that when turned on, automatically displays Web pages that have not been updated to the lastest Web standards in Compatibility view.

Cookie A small text file that a Web site stores on your computer, which contains information identifying you to the Web server and tells the Web server when you visited.

Digital certificate A part of the HTTPS protocol that identifies the URL of the Web page, the name of the certificate authority that verified the Web site, and the expiration date for the certificate; *also called* certificate.

Domain name The part of a URL that identifies the Web server on which the Web site is stored.

Encrypt To encode data sent over a connection so that only a Web site with the code can read it.

Extension *See* add-on.

Favorite The address of a Web page that you saved in a folder.

Favorites bar A bar below the Address bar that provides one-click access to your favorite Web pages.

Favorites Center A pane on the left of the browser window that you can open to display the saved favorites, the history list, and saved newsfeeds.

Feed *See* newsfeed.

History A list of the pages you have opened and the order in which you have viewed them.

Home page The main page around which a Web site is built, or the first page that opens when you start a browser. *See also* start page.

HTTP *See* hypertext transfer protocol.

HTTPS *See* hypertext transfer protocol secure.

Hypertext transfer protocol (HTTP) The standard that all computers on the Web use to communicate with each other.

Hypertext transfer protocol secure (HTTPS) The standard that computers on the Web use to communicate with each other securely; it requires that Web pages that are secure have a digital certificate and transmit encrypted data.

IE *See* Windows Internet Explorer.

InPrivate Browsing A feature of Internet Explorer 8 that allows you to open a new browser window and surf the Web without recording anything in the History list, storing files in the Temporary Internet Files folder, or recording cookies.

InPrivate Filtering A feature of Internet Explorer 8 that analyzes the content on Web pages you visit, and if the same content is used on several Web sites that you visit, allows you to block that content.

Instant Search box *See* Search box.

Internet A collection of networks that connects computers all over the world.

Internet Explorer (IE) *See* Windows Internet Explorer.

Keyword A word you type to describe the content you want to find; a search provider searches for pages that contain the keyword. *See also* search expression.

Link Text or a graphic formatted so that when you click it, another Web page loads in the browser window, you jump to another location on the same Web page, or you open a document stored on your computer or on a Web server.

Load The action of a Web page appearing in a browser window.

Newsfeed Content that is frequently updated and sent to your browser on a regular basis; *also called* feed.

Orientation The direction of the paper when a document is printed.

Path Specifies a Web page's exact location and its filename on the Web server.

Phishing site A Web site set up to look like another Web site, such as a bank's Web site, but which does not actually belong to the organization portrayed in the site; the site is set up for the purpose of illegally obtaining personal or financial information; *also called* spoofed site.

Plug-in *See* add-on.

Pop-up A new browser window that a Web site tries to open on your computer, usually without your permission. Pop-ups sometimes contain advertisements.

Pop-up Blocker A feature of Internet Explorer 8 that allows you to control the behavior of pop-ups.

Print Preview A view in Internet Explorer that shows you how the current Web page will look when it is printed.

Progress bar The area of the status bar that indicates how much of a Web page has been loaded by filling with green as the page loads.

Protocol An agreed upon standard.

Really Simple Syndication *See* RSS.

Refresh To reload content in a browser window.

Results *See* search results.

RSS (Really Simple Syndication) The format that Web sites use to provide a newsfeed.

Search box A box to the right of the Address bar in which you can type a search expression to search the Web for pages containing the keywords you typed.

Search engine *See* search provider.

Search expression A keyword or phrase you type to describe the content you want to find; a search provider searches for pages that contain the keyword.

Search provider A Web site that searches the Web for pages that contain the search expression you type; *also called* search engine.

Search results Links to Web pages displayed by a search provider that match a search expression; *also called* results.

Search results page The Web page displayed by a search provider after conducting a search; it lists links to Web pages that match the search expression.

SmartScreen Filter A feature of Internet Explorer 8 that checks to see if the Web site you are visiting is a phishing site.

Spoofed site *See* phishing site.

Start page The first page that opens when you start a browser. *See also* home page.

Status bar An area at the bottom of the browser window that displays information about the current operation.

Surf *See* browse.

Tab The area of the browser window in which Web pages appear.

tab group A collection of related tabs that are all colored with the same color.

Tabbed browsing A method of browsing the Internet that allows you to open multiple Web pages in tabs in a single browser window.

Third-party content Content on Web pages provided by companies other than the company or person who owns the Web page.

Toolbar An area of a program window that contains buttons you can click to execute common commands.

Top-level domain (TLD) A two- or three-letter identifier that indicates the type of Web site or company behind the Web site.

Uniform Resource Locator (URL)   The address of a Web page.

URL   *See* Uniform Resource Locator.

Web   *See* World Wide Web.

Web browser (browser)   Software that allows you to navigate to, open, view, and interact with files on the Web.

Web page   A specially formatted file designed for use on the Web.

Web server   A computer or a network of computers that stores Web pages and makes them available on the Web.

Web site   A collection of related Web pages stored on a Web server.

Web slice   Content that is frequently updated and sent to your browser on a regular basis.

Windows Internet Explorer (IE)   A program used to examine and interact with files on the World Wide Web; *also called* Internet Explorer.

Wizard   A series of dialog boxes that takes you step by step through a process.

World Wide Web (WWW or **Web)**   A subset of the Internet composed of files in a special format that allows them to be connected to each other.

WWW   *See* World Wide Web.

Index

home pages. *See also* Web pages
    changing, 7
    described, **2**, 4
Hotmail, 14, 39
HTML (HyperText Markup Language), 15
HTTP (Hypertext Transfer Protocol), 2
HTTPS (HyperText Transfer Protocol,
    Secure), 50

▶ I

Import/Export Settings wizard, 36
InPrivate browsing, 46–47
InPrivate filtering, 43, 46–47
InPrivate status indicator, 6–7
Instant Search box, 30–31
Internet, 2
Internet Explorer browser (Microsoft).
    See also browsers
    described, **1**
    exiting, 20–21
    starting, **4–5**
    window, elements of, 6–7
Internet Options dialog box, 20, 43, 45

▶ K

keywords, **2**

▶ L

links. *See* URLs (Uniform Resource Locators)
Live Search, 30–31, 38–41

▶ M

Manage Add-Ons dialog box, 36–37
maps, 39
marketing companies, 45
Maximize button, 4
Microsoft Internet Explorer. *See* Internet
    Explorer browser (Microsoft)
Microsoft Silverlight, 36
Microsoft Web site, 12, 20, 42

▶ N

New Tab button, **6–7**, 12
newsfeeds
    described, **40–41**
    properties, changing, 41
notification window, 44

▶ P

passwords, 43
paths, 2
PDF (Portable Document Format), 36
phishing sites, 44–45
plug-ins. *See* add-ons
Pop-up Blocker, 48–49
pop-ups, managing, **48–49**
Print button, 7
Print dialog box, 16–17
Print Preview, 16–17
printing
    graphics, 16
    help topics, 19
    orientation, 17
    text, 16
    Web pages, **16–17**
privacy policies, 47
Privacy Policy dialog box, 47
progress bar, **8**
protocols
    described, **2**
    HTTP, 2
    HTTPS, 50

▶ Q

Quick Launch toolbar, 4, 5

▶ R

Read Mail button, 7
Recently Closed Tabs command, 13
Recycle Bin, 34
Refresh All command, 13
Refresh button, 8
Refresh command, 13
Reopen Closed Tab command, 13
RSS (Really Simple Syndication), **40–41**

▶ S

Safety button, 7, 44, 46, 47
Save As dialog box, 14
saving Web pages, 14–15
Search box, **6–7**, 30–31, 46
search engines, 2
search expressions, **30–31**
search providers, 2
search results page, **30–31**
security
    certificates and, 50–51
    checking, 50–51
    passwords, 43
    privacy policies, 47
servers, 2
Set Up Windows Internet Explorer 8 wizard
    dialog box, 4
Shockwave, 36–37
shopping carts, 50–51
SmartScreen filter, 4, **44–45**
spoofed sites. *See* phishing sites
Start button, 4
Start menu, 5
start pages. *See* home pages
status bar, 6–7
Suggested Sites button, 4
Suggested Sites feature, 4, 42–43

▶ T

tab(s)
    active, **12**
    closing, 20–21
    described, **6–7**
    favorites and, 32
    groups, **12**
    settings, 20
tabbed browsing, **12–13**
temporary Internet files, 43, 46
text
    files, saving Web pages as, 15
    printing, 16
third-party content, **46**
TLDs (top-level domains), **2–3**
Tools button, 20, 48
translations, 39

►U

Ungroup This Tab command, 12–13
URLs (Uniform Resource Locators)
    anatomy of, 2–3
    Address bar and, 6
    described, **2**
    Favorites and, 10
    finding Web sites and, 8
    help for, 18–19
    security and, 50
    sending Web pages as, 14
    SmartScreen filter and, 44–45

►V

video players, 36
View Full Width button, 16, 17

►W

Web. *See* World Wide Web
Web archive files, 15
Web pages. *See also* home pages; Web sites
    described, **2–3**
    checking the security of, 50–51
    navigating to previously visited, 10–11
    saving, **14–15**

Web servers, **2**
Web slices, 7, **40–41**
Web sites. *See also* Web pages
    described, **2–3**
    finding, 8–9
    navigating, 8–9
Windows Live, 14, 39
wizards
    described, **4**
    Import/Export Settings wizard, 36
    Set Up Windows Internet Explorer 8
        wizard dialog box, 4
World Wide Web, **2–3**. *See also* Web pages;
    Web sites